Contents

Introduction

'1914 is the end of history and the beginning of modern times.' (Sellers and Yeatman, *1066 and all that*).

The First World War changed Europe almost beyond recognition. If one of the men killed in the early battles of 1914 had returned to life at the moment of the armistice on the Western Front on 11 November 1918 he would have found even the battlefield itself changed. Barbed wire, machine guns and poison gas had made the war in the West more static, and more deadly than any previous conflict. The tanks and aeroplanes, which were going to revolutionise warfare still further in the next two decades, had been used for the first time. Had the ghostly veteran tried to return home he would have had more surprises. The money in his pocket would have been greatly reduced in value, the young were less respectful, and women's clothes had changed. The behaviour of governments, particularly their attitude towards economic matters, had also been changed during the war. Revolutions at the end of the war were to bring about still more radical change. Some countries ceased to exist altogether under the terms of the post-war peace settlements.

The legacy of the First World War was to overshadow Europe for the next two decades, and almost none of the events described in this book can be understood without reference to this legacy. Leaders of the western powers had often disregarded the interests of fighting men while the war continued, but after the war they depended on soldiers, and veterans, to suppress revolution. Soldiers were also a crucial electoral constituency and veterans' organisations became important sources of influence. Generals who had made their reputation during the war (Hindenburg, Luddendorff, Pétain) played politics in the inter-war period. More strikingly non commissioned officers such as Mussolini and Hitler began to lead political organisations. Such men often provided the leadership of the fascist movements. A whole political mythology grew up around the First World War veterans; the front soldiers in Germany, the *poilus* in France, the tommies in England. The war became a symbol of national unity, comradeship and patriotism. This mythological legacy was to prove astonishingly durable: in the early 1980s Harold Macmillan (a veteran of the Somme) referred to striking Yorkshire miners as 'the men who beat the Kaiser.'

The war left a legacy of casualties: in Germany 2 million men were killed by the war; in France the figure was 1.3 million. A Frenchman who reached the age of twenty in 1914 stood a one in five chance of being dead by 1919. Casualties fell particularly heavily on two groups. The first of these was the landed aristocracy, which provided many of the junior officers who lead men into battle. The second was the peasantry of continental Europe, who provided many of the rank and file soldiers: 42% of French casualties came from this group. The industrial working classes suffered less severely than the peasantry because governments eventually realised that they needed to shelter workers in order to maintain armaments production. One result of this was that soldiers often resented what they saw as the workers' privileged status and proved all too willing to suppress the strikes, riots and revolutions that broke out in many parts of Europe in 1919; a lasting hostility to the organised working class encouraged many ex-soldiers to support the extreme right in the 1920s and 1930s.

The legacy of wartime casualties constrained much of what European governments did during the inter-war period. The payment of pensions to veterans, and to those crippled, widowed and orphaned by the war, drained resources. There were 360,000 war widows drawing pensions in Germany in 1924; half of all French government spending during the late 1930s went on war pensions and repayment of interest on war loans. These burdens help to account for the German government's inability to control public spending during the Weimar period and for the French government's inability to rearm effectively before the Second World War. France was also weakened by the fact that its birth rate had dropped to half its normal level during the war. This meant that during the late 1930s France entered the so-called 'empty years' when it lacked an adequate cohort of men eligible for military service. This partly accounted for France's fear of confrontation with Germany.

The First World War also left an economic legacy. Before 1914 European currencies had been fixed to the gold standard. The value of money and interest rates were remarkably stable. Governments financed much of the war by borrowing or by printing money, the result was inflation. Inflation hit rentiers (i.e. people who lived off fixed incomes and savings) particularly badly. However, not everyone lost from inflation. Workers had few savings and their wages sometimes rose faster than prices because their labour was perceived to be necessary to the war effort. People who had had debts before 1914 also often benefited from inflation as they were able to make repayments in valueless currency. The German peasantry, who had frequently borrowed to modernize, drew particular benefits from inflation – though they sometimes lost from investing their gains in war bonds that subsequently turned out to be worthless. Dealing with the consequences of wartime monetary policy occupied much time in every European country. This was seen most clearly in Germany where inflation was exacerbated by the consequences of resistance to French invasion of the Ruhr. The restoration of pre-war money values became a symbol of national prestige. Winston Churchill's return to the Gold Standard, the French defence of the 'Franc Poincaré' between 1928 and 1936, and Mussolini's 1926 revaluation of the lira were all designed to win such prestige.

The First World War overshadowed events for two decades, but this does not mean that the history of inter-war Europe can simply be understood in terms of the unfolding legacy of the war. Events often moved in a direction that no one could have foreseen in the aftermath of 1919. New technologies changed Europe in ways that would not have been conceivable in 1919. The most obvious of these concerned the conduct of warfare itself. Aeroplanes and tanks meant that the battle of France in 1940 was as different from the First World War as the First World War had been to the Franco-Prussian war. As important as the actual use to which military technologies were put was the expectation that surrounded such technologies. Many Europeans expected that aerial bombing would prove even more destructive than it did, and Stanley Baldwin's phrase 'the bomber will always get through' haunted statesmen during the 1930s. Technologies also had more passive applications. Motor car manufacture developed on a large scale in this period, and this industry pioneered new techniques based on the production line (in which work was broken down into a series of simple tasks). The huge car factories of Fiat in Turin or Renault in Paris also became the centres of labour relations conflict. Motor cars became associated with prosperity and freedom; they began to transform patterns of bourgeois leisure and when the Nazis looked for a symbol of their success they hit on the idea of making a 'people's car'. New technology also began to transform politics. Hitler and Mussolini used radio and cinema to transmit their staged rallies and speeches; Chamberlain used the same techniques with equal skill to convey his reassuring chats; Charles de Gaulle (exiled leader of the Free French from 1940 to 1944) was soon to become the first national leader to be known to his people almost exclusively through radio broadcasts.

Economic development also influenced politics between the wars. Many industries saw a drive for rationalisation of production during the 1920s as production line techniques and the ideas about piece work and time and motion studies of the American engineer, Taylor, were implemented. Most importantly, the world depression that began with the Wall Street Crash of 1929 dominated politics in all European countries. Depression produced political upheaval. Men, like Mosley in England and Déat in France, lost faith in conventional economics and eventually lost faith in conventional politics as they drifted towards fascism. Mass unemployment in Germany helped to weaken the Weimar Republic: it increased working class support for the Communist Party and increased the support of a middle class, which had already been hit by inflation and stabilisation during the 1920s, for Nazism. The depression did not have identical effects in the various European countries. In France the depression lasted a long time (France did not recover her 1929 levels of production until after the Second World War) but it did not produce social crisis. Official levels of unemployment never exceeded half a million. Germany and Great Britain, by contrast, both experienced mass unemployment, though the political consequences of this (Baldwin's 'safety first' in Britain; Hitler's Third Reich in Germany) could not have been more different.

This brief introduction has suggested that there were certain broad influences working behind European history between 1919 and 1939. However, it has also tried to stress that similar influences could produce very different results from one country to another. There were great differences between the winners and losers in the First World War (and not all of those who felt themselves to be losers lived in countries that had formally undergone defeat). There were differences between rich and poor countries. There were also striking differences within individual countries. The migrant labourers who came from the Italian South did not much care whether they found work in Le Cresot or Turin; both places seemed equally foreign. Within France average incomes, and even birth-rates, in the industrialised areas were sometimes double those found in the backward southwest. For some countries the very words inter-war are meaningless. Spain, Switzerland and Sweden did not participate in either of the two wars. Even the inhabitants of the countries that attract most attention did not always experience the inter-war period as one of crisis and depression. In this period Germany is usually seen as an aggressive and dangerous power, but Stresemann won the Nobel peace prize in 1926. France is seen as an economic failure, but the Bank of France helped to prop up the English financial system in the early 1930s. English rulers are seen as weak and despicable appeasers, but Baldwin received an ecstatic send-off from parliament when he resigned as prime minister in 1937 (his last act was to raise MPs' wages). Furthermore, the lives of ordinary people were not always dominated by the political and military events that make up conventional history: even A. J. P. Taylor spent much of the late 1930s worrying about the state of his vegetable garden.

PART I
The Post-War Settlement

The peace settlement that brought the First World War to a close has had a bad press. As Alan Sharp stresses, the most important treaty (that signed at Versailles, on 28 June 1919, to deal with Germany) was concluded in haste and confusion. E. H. Carr's book on European diplomacy, written just before the outbreak of the Second World War in 1939, was particularly hard on the Versailles treaty:

> Woodrow Wilson, the impassioned admirer of Bright and Gladstone, transplanted the nineteenth-century rationalist faith to the almost virgin soil of international politics and, bringing it back with him to Europe gave it a new lease of life. Nearly all popular theories of international politics between the two world wars were reflexions, seen in an American mirror, of nineteenth-century liberal thought.[1]

There is some justice in Carr's analysis. The peace settlement of 1919 contained some naïve provisions. It established a League of Nations that possessed no means to enforce its will. It even created the International Labour Organisation where representatives from countries such as China, which was gripped by civil war, solemnly advised their European colleagues on the need to establish eight hour days and to suppress child labour. However, if Woodrow Wilson was a naïve nineteenth-century liberal, the other major figures to participate in drawing up the peace settlement were nothing of the sort. Georges Clemenceau, prime minister of France, was an almost psychopathically ruthless man: he had had strikers shot, his political opponent harried from office, and even arranged for his own wife to be imprisoned. Clemenceau wanted to see changes within France that would have produced a more presidential style of government. He had overseen experiments with economic interventionism during the war and some of his lieutenants, such as André Tardieu, wished to see a more organised economy continued into peacetime. If Clemenceau had not been defeated in the presidential election of 1920, it is possible that the implementation of such ideas might have made France into a stronger power and perhaps have prevented the Versailles system from breaking down with the German occupation of the Rhineland in 1936.

David Lloyd George, the English prime minister of 1919, had

some ideas that were similar to Clemenceau's. He was also a tough and energetic character who wished to see his country run in new ways but, like Clemenceau, he was pushed out of power soon after the signature of Versailles and then criticised British policy from the sidelines for much of the inter-war period. Even the much maligned President Wilson was not in a position to implement his policies after he returned from Versailles. One of Wilson's guiding principles was that foreign policy should be controlled by parliaments rather than by unaccountable rulers but, just as parliaments had rejected Clemenceau and Lloyd George, so the American Congress refused to accept Wilson's dream of an America that would intervene more actively in European affairs and turned instead towards isolationism.

The result of the confusion during the negotiations and the changes of leadership after them was that the Versailles settlement did not fit in with the intentions of any of those involved. The long-term effects of these confusions are the subject of debate. At the time, many liberal minded people (particularly in England) believed that the treaty was excessively harsh towards Germany. This feeling was exacerbated by hostility to the French that had grown up during the war. The poet Robert Graves, who had been a junior officer on the western front, wrote in his autobiography that he would be unwilling to fight again – except against the French. Helping Germans against the French was the first of the many quixotic projects to engage the attention of Graham Greene. The most famous statement of English liberal hostility to Versailles was by the economist Maynard Keynes. His *The Economic Consequences of the Peace* alleged that the reparations imposed on Germany would prove impossible to pay. Other commentators have pointed to the clauses of the Versailles treaty that placed guilt for starting the war on the Germans as a source of bitterness for right-wingers in Germany.

However, there were others who believed that the Versailles treaty was too soft on the Germans. Some French generals, such as Foch and Mangin, wanted France to exercise permanent control of the Rhineland. A French economist, Etienne Mantoux wrote *The Carthaginian Peace of the Economic Consequences of Mr Keynes* in which he alleged that Germany had never in fact paid more than a trivial sum in reparations. Recent research has tended to vindicate the French rather than the British. Fritz Fisher and his associates have argued that the Germans were indeed responsible for the outbreak of war in 1914 and that they, too, would have sought to impose annexations and reparations on their defeated enemies. Economic historians now argue that the economic weakness of Weimar Germany came not from the burden of reparations but from excessive government spending: taxes in Germany in 1925 took 15% of national income as against 8% in 1913, reparations never amounted to more than 3%. Most importantly, the damage of the post-war peace settlements came not so much from Versailles as from the treaties of St Germain and Trianon that dealt with the Austro-Hungarian Empire. These treaties ensured that a weakened Germany was surrounded by the temptations of even more weakened small states in Eastern and Central Europe: in this context the conflict that broke out in 1939 might be seen as the inevitable war of the Habsburg succession.

Note

(1) Carr, E. H. *The Twenty Years' Crisis 1919–39. An Introduction to the Study of International Relations* (Macmillan, 1939) p. 27.

Alan Sharp
Versailles 1919:
'A Tragedy of Disappointment'

The Versailles settlement at the end of the First World War has long been seen as fatally flawed. Alan Sharp, however, draws attention to the appalling difficulties that faced those who framed it.

The peace settlement at the end of the First World War takes its name from the treaty which the main defeated power, Germany, signed in Louis XIV's palace at Versailles on 28 June 1919. This is appropriate because it was the need to discover a solution to the 'German problem' – whether this powerful industrial and military state could be accommodated into a peaceful structure of international relations – which dominated the proceedings. There were four other treaties signed in palaces scattered about the Parisian suburbs: St Germain (Austria); Neuilly (Bulgaria); Trianon (Hungary) and Sèvres (Turkey). The treaty with Turkey was renegotiated after Mustapha Kemal's successful revolution and signed at Lausanne in Switzerland on 24 July 1923. The process of peacemaking thus lasted longer than the war itself.

The Versailles settlement has been condemned as a failure, an inadequate answer to the world's problems in 1919 which sowed the seeds of future conflict. This is not entirely fair. It was because the great powers had started a war in 1914 that over 30 Allied and associated powers gathered to make peace in 1919. Four years of industrialised warfare on an unprecedented scale had solved few problems, made many worse and created new ones. Desperate to win, or to avoid defeat, the states involved resorted to new and terrible weapons, they bribed potential allies, attempted to undermine the stability and morale of their opponents by propaganda and promises and encouraged the flagging efforts of their own populations by offering visions of a post-war world which would justify the present sacrifice. The war killed perhaps 8 to 10 million soldiers, cost some £24,000,000,000, destroyed the Russian, Austro-Hungarian, Ottoman and German empires leaving central and eastern Europe, the Balkans and the Near and Middle East without their traditional rulers. It distorted economies and helped to create revolutions, famine and epidemics. The fighting and dying did not cease with the Armistice on 11 November 1918. If the destination

Key
Territorial transfers by
the Peace Treaties

from Germany

from Austria-Hungary

from Russia

from Bulgaria

demilitarised
Rhineland zone

NORWAY

FINLAND

SWEDEN

ESTONIA

LATVIA

RUSSIA

LITHUANIA

Memel

DANZIG

Northern
Schleswig

DENMARK

EAST
PRUSSIA

NETHERLANDS

Polish
Corridor

Posen

POLAND

GERMANY

Ruhr

BELGIUM

Upper
Silesia

Eupen-
Malmedy

Saar

LUX

Alsace-
Lorraine

CZECHOSLOVAKIA

R. Rhine

SWITZERLAND

AUSTRIA

HUNGARY

RUMANIA

FRANCE

YUGOSLAVIA

R. Danube

ITALY

BULGARIA

ALBANIA

TURKEY

GREECE

0   300 miles

0   400 km

The Versailles Peace Settlement, 1919

was a stable and peaceful world then, as the old Irish story has it, 1919 was not the ideal point of departure.

Wilson's peace programme

Into this desperate situation the American President, Woodrow Wilson, had injected hope in a series of speeches in 1918 analysing Europe's problems and offering remedies. As a liberal manifesto it would be hard to better the Fourteen Points of 8 January, Four Principles of 11 February, Four Ends of 4 July and Five Particulars of 27 September even if the cynical French Premier, Georges Clemenceau, sneered that God had needed only Ten Points. Wilson believed that the war had arisen from secret alliances and the frustrated aspirations of national groupings trapped in the European empires of Germany, Austria-Hungary and Russia, all autocracies that gave their peoples no political authority. His remedies were national self-determination and democracy within a reformist capitalist system and he proposed to allow the same scope for public opinion to influence governments in international relations by his League of Nations, designed to introduce open diplomacy and time for reflection to avoid another precipitate rush to war like July 1914. In the pre-Armistice agreement with Germany, 5 November 1918, the Allies committed themselves to translating their 'programme of the world's peace' from propaganda into a workable settlement. Wilson, however, already feared by December 1918 that he had raised too many expectations and that the result of the conference would be a 'tragedy of disappointment'.

The organisation of the conference

Wilson's concern was justified by events. The conference found itself trying to do too many things at once, partly because of poor management, partly because everything was happening at once. The conference opened on 18 January: issues at the time included whether it was to establish terms for dictation to the Germans without debate, or to agree its positions, and then invite the Germans to negotiate? Would neutrals be invited eventually to discuss wider issues, rather as the Congress of Vienna in 1815 had followed the Paris meetings of 1814? It was dominated by the political leaders of three of the five victorious great powers: Clemenceau of France, Wilson of the United States and David Lloyd George of Great Britain. The Japanese were interested mainly in the Pacific and played little part. Italy's dubious credentials as a great power and Prime Minister Vittorio Orlando's poor grasp of English left it on the fringes of the game. It was held in Paris, which was sensible in that the city had the hotels and bureaucratic support necessary to service a conference of over 1,000 delegates, but where the strong feeling against Germany was not helpful.

The crisis of the conference

By late March there was a serious threat that the conference would collapse through inertia. The Council of Ten, two representatives, usually the premier and foreign minister, from each of the five major powers, had dominated the first two months but it was too unwieldy. At its last meeting on 24 March there were over 50 people present, significantly still discussing a problem raised at the first meeting. Drafts of a Covenant for the League of Nations and the German disarmament terms existed and Germany's colonies were forfeited but little else was clear, except that the terms would be dictated, not negotiated and there would be no wider gathering. It was replaced by private meetings between Clemenceau, Lloyd George, Wilson and Orlando, the Council of Four. At first they met with only an interpreter, later with a secretary to record their decisions, reached after consulting a wide variety of advisers. They worked under tremendous pressure and without an ordered agenda, their decisions were often arbitrary, based on imperfect information or political expediency, but they did decide matters, though the enforceability of those decisions diminished as the distance from Paris increased. It was none-too-soon. There were problems everywhere: the frontiers of Germany and France in the Saar and Rhineland; the wider issue of French security; Polish access to the Baltic and the sovereignty of Danzig; reparations; Anglo-French squabbles over the Middle East. In the background were Italian territorial claims; Australian, South African, New Zealand and Japanese demands for Germany's colonies, and Greek ambitions in the Near East where the Ottoman Empire had collapsed. Each of these questions was both separate and part of a whole, complicated in its own right and further complicated because it fitted into an ill-matching jigsaw of worldwide allied inter-relationships, fears and ambitions. Furthermore, Wilson believed there was a race between peace and anarchy and that, unless peace was concluded quickly, he would lose his tug-of-war for the soul of the world to his main – if absent – rivals, Lenin and the Bolsheviks.

The Four, soon reduced to three by Orlando's withdrawal, frustrated over Fiume, produced a settlement in a hectic six-week period, inevitably striking deals, compromising ideals and disappointing aspirations. The cumulative effect of their individual decisions was not necessarily what they had intended though Wilson convinced himself that the essentials of his programme survived this process. Many of his erstwhile admirers felt that he had betrayed their trust, outwitted by Clemenceau and Lloyd George.

National self-determination

Two issues at the conference caused special disappointment – national self-determination and reparations. Both sides had risked the double-edged weapon of nationalism, now the conference had to fulfil expectations which were not confined to nationalities controlled by the losers. Warned that the idea was 'a principle loaded with dynamite' Wilson later admitted there were many more nationalities in Europe seeking independence than he realised. Typically his ideas were confused. The Fourteen Points spoke of recreating Poland from territory that was 'indisputably Polish' and of allowing her 'free and secure access' to the Baltic. Yet this could be achieved only by depriving Germany of indisputably German territory to create a corridor to Danzig, an indisputably German port.

The successful nationalities were the swiftest to react in 1918 – the Poles, the Czechs and the founders of Yugoslavia. The conference did not create these new states, it recognised them and adjudicated between them. Disappointment was inevitable, particularly in eastern Europe and the Balkans where invasions, migrations and historical accident had created a bewildering kaleidoscope of races and religions. In case after case the ethnic arguments were confused even before considering practical problems like the economic and military viability of frontiers and the location of vital roads and railways, all complicated by the exaggerated demands of the disputing claimants. Most of the available statistics were unreliable and interested parties drew their maps with care – 'A perverted map was a life-belt to many a floundering argument' declared one expert. Each consideration produced a different frontier; the only consistency was that they never matched and hence it was easy to find inconsistency in the decisions finally reached. If one of the great powers had a direct interest the difficulties were compounded. The return of Alsace-Lorraine to France was inevitable and indeed, uniquely amongst the territorial rearrangements is stated by the treaty to date from 11 November 1918, but France wanted more. Fearing the industrial strength and demographic superiority of Germany, the French argued that the Rhineland should be detached from Germany and either given to France or made independent, thus providing France with a military frontier on, or beyond, the Rhine. She sought also the German coal-producing area of the Saar to replace the mines sabotaged by the retreating Germans and to meet the increased demand from Alsace-Lorraine. Some dubious ethnic arguments were advanced but no one took them seriously; this was a clash between the perceived security and economic requirements of France and the principle of national self-determination. It worried Lloyd George in particular. Fearing a German revolution or refusal to sign, he argued eloquently against transferring too many Germans to France, Poland or even Denmark. As a young man visiting Paris he had been moved by the black drapes over the statue representing Strasbourg, symbol of the lost provinces of Alsace-Lorraine, and he pleaded with the conference not to create unnecessary German Alsace-Lorraines in reverse.

The conference produced some ingenious devices to escape these problems. Lloyd George and Wilson offered military guarantees to France if she would abandon a detached Rhineland. After exacting further concessions, particularly the creation of a demilitarised zone on both sides of the Rhine and an Allied occupation for 15 years, Clemenceau agreed. The Anglo-Americans later defaulted on their guarantees. France needed the Saar and Poland needed Danzig but, whilst they were granted, respectively, the coal and the use of the port, it was the League of Nations that assumed responsibility for the government of both areas. Plebiscites were sometimes held to determine the wishes of the inhabitants, though these could produce surprising results (as in Allenstein where a Polish-speaking population voted to remain German) or even, as in Upper Silesia, further confuse the situation. The League was asked to protect minorities left on the wrong side of some of the new boundaries but with mixed results. The settlement reduced the 60 million people of 1914 living in a state in which they were not the dominant nationality to 30 million in 1919, but the 1919 minorities were probably more discontented than those of 1914. Within almost all the new states there were groups who did not want to be there and who often looked to a neighbouring state for protection. The opportunities for a sufficiently powerful discontented state to disrupt the new order were obvious; Hitler's 1938 exploitation of the ex-Austrian Sudeten Germans in Czechoslovakia is a classic example.

Reparations

If national self-determination created the most disappointment it was reparations which most undermined the moral credibility of the settlement, particularly after J. M. Keynes published his stinging attack, *The Economic Consequences of the Peace*, in December 1919. The allies had undertaken not to demand their full war costs from Germany yet, with the exception of the United States, they did so. The French and British peoples expected Germany to pay and, despite vigorous American objections, Clemenceau and Lloyd

George feared to disappoint them. Eventually a disastrous face-saving formula was discovered which stated that Germany was responsible for the war and hence liable for its entire cost (Article 231, the 'War Guilt' clause) but, because she could not afford this, the Allies would limit (under Article 232) their demands to the reparation of damages to civilians and their property. Controversially the definition of civilian damage included separation allowances to soldiers' families and pensions to wounded soldiers and their dependants because soldiers were 'merely civilians in uniform.' Wilson admitted that this was illogical but probably believed that the treaty would determine a total sum to discharge Germany's debts based on an estimate of what she could afford. The categories of damage would thus not affect the sum required but would ensure a fairer distribution of the proceeds. Rather than France and Belgium getting almost everything, Britain and her Dominions would at least receive something. Thus he accepted this dubious proposition which eventually doubled the demands made on Germany. The allies could not agree upon a lump sum which they thought their voters would accept; instead the Germans in 1919 were told only for which headings they would have to pay – a rather different German 'blank cheque' to that of July 1914. In May 1921 the Reparation Commission assessed Germany's liability at 132 thousand million gold marks (£6,600,000,000), two to three times the sum Keynes thought reasonable. Older accounts emphasised French greed and need as the reasons for the failure to reach a practical reparations deal but more recently Britain has been criticised for making the most extreme demands and preventing a settlement. The Americans too have been attacked for not admitting some linkage between reparations and repayment of money borrowed from her by her allies during the war. No one emerged with much credit (literal or metaphorical) from this shabby episode which created bitterness between the Allies and in Germany.

Conclusion

The settlement neither crippled Germany nor reconciled her to the new order; instead it left her with grievances and the latent potential to make trouble. It based its judgements on three premises: that Germany had started the war; that she had fought a dirty war; and that she had lost. Accepting none of these the Germans believed the settlement was unjust – why were the Germans of Austria, the Sudetenland, the Polish corridor and Danzig, even of Alsace-Lorraine and Schleswig, denied national self-determination? Why were the German forces limited to a tiny navy and an army of 100,000 men when no such restrictions were imposed on her neighbours? Why should she lose 13% and 10% of her pre-war territory and population, all her colonies and suffer occupation? Her former leaders claimed (with remarkable success) that the new democratic regime had stabbed her in the back – hardly an auspicious omen. Reparations were monstrous, the losses of eastern territory unjustifiable and the demands that she surrender her war leaders for trial shameful; in short a 'slave treaty'. Set against this, however, must be the settlement a victorious Germany might have imposed, if her treaties with Rumania (Bucharest) and Russia (Brest-Litovsk) were accurate previews.

Other powers were also dissatisfied, most justifiably Hungary which lost two-thirds of her land and 59% of her people, and Russia which lost territory without even being at the conference. Even the winners wanted more: the Italians were disappointed over the Adriatic settlement; the Poles and Czechs fell out over Teschen; the Balkan powers all looked jealously at each other's gains; the French were satisfied, but only to the extent that they believed that more desirable outcomes were unattainable. They remained terrified of Germany but kept provoking her. Britain, which wanted to leave Europe to its own devices, rapidly developed a bad conscience over the whole affair, and tended to believe the Germans when they said they could not execute the treaty; the French remained convinced the Germans could, but would not.

Foch, the French commander of the Allied armies, condemned the treaty as 'an Armistice for 20 years'. His verdict proved uncannily accurate but was not inevitable. Any fair judgement must consider the reasons why there had been a war in 1914, the difficult circumstances of 1919, and the performance of those who governed Europe after the peace had been made. Even if the settlement was a 'tragedy of disappointment' it was as much because of its virtues as its faults. It did not destroy Germany, it tried to draw its maps around people and, through the League, to create a more just and successful international system. Perhaps a post-Cold War generation of historians, who will live through a new attempt to reshape Europe, will have more sympathy with the immensity of the task facing the peacemakers in Paris in 1919. Small wonder that Wilson should lament 'What is expected of me only God could perform.'

Alan Sharp is a lecturer in History at the University of Ulster at Coleraine.

Anthony Lentin
The Consequences of the Versailles Settlement

Any peace settlement, if it is to succeed, has to be enforceable, and it has to be enforced. Anthony Lentin examines the consequences of the peace-making at Versailles and the extent to which there was either the will or the capacity amongst the allies to enforce and defend the settlement reached.

Versailles came as a stunning blow to German pride. There was no negotiation between Germany and the Allies. The treaty was simply presented for Germany 'to sign or not to sign' – in German eyes a *Diktat*. Versailles deprived Germany of well over 10% of its population, territory and economic resources. Germany lost its entire colonial empire, all its territorial gains made in the war, and its own long-standing possessions: Alsace-Lorraine, Eupen-Malmédy and Northern Schleswig, the province of Posen and the 'Polish Corridor', half of Upper Silesia, and the German ports of Danzig and Memel. It placed the Rhineland and Saar under Allied and League of Nations control respectively, the Rhineland being designated a demilitarised zone, out of bounds to German forces in perpetuity. The German army was disbanded and disarmed. The high seas fleet and merchant navy were confiscated. Germany was saddled with liability to pay reparations for all war-damage suffered by the Allies, and under the 'war-guilt' clause – with responsibility for the war, which was attributed to her 'aggression'. Not surprisingly, Versailles provoked vehement resentment and hostility in Germany. This was among the first and most lasting of its consequences.

Despite these draconian terms, however, Germany's geopolitical status, compared both to what it had been in 1914 and to that of its neighbours in 1919, was potentially buoyant. Germany remained the dominant power in a Europe exhausted and diminished by war. Versailles did not weaken Germany as much as the war had weakened her European enemies. Unlike devastated France, Belgium, Poland or Serbia, Germany emerged from Versailles not only physically undamaged but strategically much advantaged. Gone were the 1914 barriers to German expansionism in the east and south: the empires of Russia and Austria-Hungary. Instead Germany was fringed by the new, untried, national succession-states sanctioned at Versailles: Poland, Czechoslovakia, Austria, the

Baltic states. Relative to Germany they were small, or, like Poland, over-extended and disunited, with dissident minorities, including Germans. Instead of combining to resist German pressure, nearly all these states were bitterly at odds among themselves over disputed boundaries and populations.

This fragmentation (or 'balkanisation') of Central and Eastern Europe at Versailles brought chronic destabilisation to the area and a corresponding increase in German influence, especially economic and commerical. Unimpaired by the war and now without colonial distractions, German manufacturing interests dominated these neighbouring states, and permeated the Balkans themselves. In this traditionally turbulent peninsula, Serbia (enlarged into Yugoslavia) and an expanded Rumania squabbled among themselves and with truncated, revisionist Hungary and Bulgaria. The one tower of strength in central, east and south-east Europe after Versailles was Germany.

The Allies' adoption of national self-determination at Versailles thus created a European power-vacuum conducive to German expansionism. The application of the principle at the expense of Germans, especially in Poland, rekindled a sense of racial pride in Germany and a heightened awareness of kith and kin outside its borders. These *Auslandsdeutsche* (Germans abroad) included not only Germans now unwillingly domiciled in Poland, Alsace-Lorraine or Eupen-Malmédy, but also Germans who had never belonged to Imperial Germany, notably 7 million Austrians and 2½ million 'Sudeten' Germans in Czechoslovakia. The gathering of such *Auslandsdeutsche* within an expanded 'Greater Germany', though contrary to the letter of Versailles – Austro-German union, for example, was expressly forbidden – became both a popular national aspiration and a feasible political goal in the 'balkanised' Europe of nation-states legitimated at Versailles.

France's failure in victory

In France, Versailles was met by a justified sense of vulnerability and foreboding. France's long-term security, far from being guaranteed at Versailles, was precarious as seldom before. Versailles did little to protect it from Germany and nothing to compensate its demographic inferiority. For France, the human cost of the war was proportionately higher than for any other major belligerent: one Frenchman in four under the age of 30 had been killed. 40 million Frenchmen still confronted at least 60 million Germans, who enjoyed a higher birth-rate and a younger population.

Strategically, France's prospects after 1919 were dire. It had lost a great wartime ally, Imperial Russia, whose intervention had saved her from defeat in 1914. At Versailles, in return for promises of military alliance from Lloyd George and Wilson, Clemenceau abandoned France's key demand for a strategic frontier on the Rhine. When these promises came to nothing, France was left in the lurch, without strategic protection or allied aid. Ties with Belgium and the succession-states were no substitute for alliance with Britain and America. Indeed, rather than keep Germany at bay, the client-states involved France in quarrels of their own, between Poland and Russia, for instance; and Poland seemed likely to draw France into conflict with Germany over Danzig and the Corridor. Yet France could devise no other way to protect itself from German resurgence than by guaranteeing the Versailles settlement in its entirety, an unrealistic hope without powerful allies.

In these circumstances, reparations assumed particular importance for France, not only to fund the reconstruction of its devastated north-east, but also to enable it to repay its enormous war-debts to Britain and America, which America refused to waive. Germany, unless made to contribute, would escape the financial consequences of the war, being unencumbered by external war-debts and ready to resume its pre-war export drive with a head start.

Allied disunity and disintegration

The Allies had been hard put to reach agreement at Versailles, and the coalition fell apart soon after. The United States refused to ratify either Versailles or the treaty of alliance with France. Britain, satisfied with colonial gains and with strategic and maritime security from Germany, distrusted many of the territorial provisions of the treaties. In *The Economic Consequences of the Peace* (1919), J. M. Keynes helped to turn liberal opinion in Britain and America against Versailles. German recovery, he argued, was essential to the economic well-being of Europe generally. This was an attractive doctrine in depressed post-war Britain.

France alone aspired to enforce Versailles in full, lest its fragile security evaporated completely. Yet how could France compel German submission? Initially France believed that a show of force would demonstrate to Germany (and Britain) that France meant business. In 1920, when German forces entered the demilitarised Rhineland, French contingents were sent across the Rhine in retaliation. Again, in 1923, when Germany defaulted on reparations, Prime Minister Poincaré ordered French troops into the Ruhr.

Military occupation was almost wholly counterproductive.It sparked off passive resistance and hyperinflation in Germany. More important, it profoundly alienated Britain and America, who pointedly dissociated themselves from the French action, complaining of French attempts to 'bully' Germany. America withdrew its token forces from the Rhineland. Both ex-Allies intervened between France and Germany to impose a new reparations settlement under the Dawes Plan (1924); and Britain negotiated a French withdrawal from the Ruhr and a political compromise between France and Germany by the treaty of Locarno. Both of these settlements, financial and diplomatic, derogated from Versailles, and thus objectively favoured Germany. The Dawes Plan and later the Young Plan (1929) introduced a fixed schedule of scaled-down reparation payments, financed by generous Allied loans, with the aim of building up Germany as a stable trading-partner. As a recent historian reminds us, 'the United States and to a lesser extent the European allies subsidised Germany during the Weimar era, and not the other way round.' In 1931, under pressure of the world economic crisis, reparations ceased altogether.

At Locarno, the British Foreign Secretary, Austen Chamberlain, mediated between France and Germany. Germany undertook to respect, and Britain to guarantee the demilitarised status of the Rhineland and the frontiers of France and Belgium laid down at Versailles. This appeared to answer France's security needs and to offer stability in western Europe. On the other hand, Britain refused to take responsibility for any of the other 1919 frontiers. The Polish Corridor, said Austen Chamberlain, was not worth 'the bones of a British grenadier'. By limiting its liability to France and Belgium and disclaiming any interest in eastern Europe Britain, in effect, wrote off the rest of the Versailles settlement, leaving Germany a free hand in dealing with its other neighbours.

The failure of the Ruhr episode, France's resulting diplomatic isolation, and political and financial pressure from Britain and America, produced a radical change of policy in Paris. French attempts to coerce Germany gave way to attempts at Franco-German *détente* associated with Austen Chamberlain and his French and German counterparts, Briand and Stresemann. Briand hoped to bind Germany to a modified version of Versailles by enmeshing it in a network of voluntary agreements: in 1925 Locarno, in 1926 German entry to the League of Nations, in 1928 German adherence to the Kellogg-Briand non-aggression pact.

Instead of reconciling Germany to Versailles, however, *détente* increased German impatience and accelerated demands for further revision. Continually stepping up the price of German goodwill, Stresemann pressed for Allied evacuation of the Rhineland, the return of Eupen-Malmédy, the Saar and the German colonies. His secret agenda included revised frontiers with Poland and

Czechoslovakia, the incorporation of Austria within a 'Greater Germany' and even the recovery of Alsace-Lorraine.

The Rhineland

At Versailles, Germany agreed to disarm and to replace conscription by a small professional army of 100,000 volunteers (the *Reichswehr*). Paradoxically, this enabled the military authorities to recruit from the finest applicants a magnificent fighting élite, the seedbed for the future training of a new mass army. There was also a small German navy, and in defiance of Versailles, the beginnings of an airforce. Evading treaty prohibitions on rearmament, Germany placed orders for equipment in neutral or friendly countries: Sweden, Spain, Italy and Russia. Both before and after the Russo-German treaties of Rapallo (1922) and Berlin (1926), tanks and poison-gas, forbidden to Germany at Versailles, were manufactured in the Soviet Union, which also permitted German army manoeuvres on Russian territory. An allied military inspectorate, stationed in Germany under the provisions of Versailles, could do little to control the modernisation of Germany's armed forces, and was in any case withdrawn in 1927 as part of the policy of *détente*.

One feature only of the Versailles settlement kept Germany under control: allied military occupation of the Rhineland. Occupation was the real guarantee of the peace, the key to the security both of France and the succession-states. In stipulating a maximum term of 15 years, however, Versailles also provided for its own undoing. The last allied detachments left the Rhineland in 1930, just as Germany was on the point of recovering its military strength.

Conclusion

Undermining the Versailles settlement from the start was the failure to solve the continuing threat posed by Germany's natural predominance in Europe. The victors sought to construct a new Europe of nation-states, imposed at Germany's expense and yet premised on German goodwill, or at least on joint allied readiness to maintain the peace. Neither precondition was met. French attempts to enforce Versailles did little except antagonise Britain and America as well as Germany. Anglo-French concessions at Locarno and after whetted, without satisfying, German revisionism. As soon as Germany was strong enough to challenge what remained of Versailles, the one element capable of preventing it – the Allied presence in the Rhineland – was removed.

Anthony Lentin is Reader in History at the Open University.

PART II
The Legacy of the Russian Revolution

The Russian Revolution of October 1917 is widely regarded as the most important single event of the twentieth century. It brought the Soviet Union into being, and provided an inspiration for Communist regimes and movements throughout the world. However, the interpretation outlined above overstates the significance of the October Revolution. At the end of this episode, Lenin and the Bolsheviks controlled Petrograd, but they only controlled Russia after several years of civil war. Furthermore, similar revolutions occurred in many other parts of central and eastern Europe at the end of the First World, but the revolutions launched by Bela Kun in Hungary, Rosa Luxembourg in Berlin and by Kurt Eisner in Bavaria were all put down by right-wing forces: Luxembourg and Eisner were murdered and Kun escaped to Russia (where he was killed by Stalin in 1937). In this context the key question is not so much why revolution succeeded in Russia and failed elsewhere, but why counter-revolution failed in Russia and succeeded elsewhere.

There are some purely military answers to this question: Trotsky provided the Bolsheviks with competent military leadership, and the centralisation of communications around Petrograd hampered their opponents. There are also three broader reasons for the different outcome of revolution in Russia and the rest of Europe. Firstly, the industrial working class was larger and more organised in central Europe, especially Germany, than in Russia. This had encouraged many Marxists to expect that Germany would be the birthplace of workers' revolution, but in reality the trade unions and socialist parties in Germany had become too institutionalized to be revolutionary. The German trade unions had around seven million members by 1919, they controlled large resources and their political allies were the largest party in parliament – all this meant that they had much to lose if the established order collapsed. Furthermore, the management of the war economy had increased the power of labour leaders and their willingness to co-operate with the army and industrialists. It was this tradition that underlay the pact between Ebert (the socialist leader) and Groener (a general) in November 1919. Most labour leaders sought to restrain their followers from revolution and they allowed the army to suppress outbreaks that did occur. Hostility between social democrats, who had effectively abandoned revolution, and communists who remained revolutionary and loyal to the new Third International that had been established in Moscow, was intense. Bela Kun's first revolutionary action was to attack the Budapest social democratic paper, and the animosities born in 1919 and 1920 were to make united action on the Left impossible in all European countries until 1935.

The other two groups who fought against revolution were the army and peasantry. In central Europe, urban revolutionaries were terrified of being starved out by the surrounding countryside. In Russia, by contrast, the peasantry had been alienated from the old regime by the economic impact of the First World War. The breakdown of the rail system had prevented the Russian peasantry from selling their grain, while inflation forced them to pay ever higher prices for equipment and supplies. In the face of this, many peasants simply withdrew from the market economy. Unlike their counterparts in the rest of Europe, the Russian peasants felt that they had little to gain from the protection of private property, and during the civil war they did not rally in large numbers to the counter-revolutionary forces. Indeed they sometimes joined 'Green' armies to fight against any forces (Red or White) that came into their areas. The army was another disappointment to Russian counter-revolutionaries. The comparatively mobile nature of the Eastern Front and the fact that reserve soldiers were stationed close to workers in Petrograd encouraged a breakdown of discipline in the ranks of the Russian army; the absence of a strong corps of NCOs (sergeants and corporals) meant that there was no one to restore discipline and even some officers joined the Red Army to fight for revolution. In the rest of Europe, by contrast, armies usually remained loyal to the established order: strikers and revolutionaries were put down by troops during riots in Turin in 1917 and during the disturbances in Berlin in 1919. Semi-official groups of war veterans were also organised to combat revolution in many parts of Europe: such men could be found in the Italian *Fasci*, the German *Freikorps* or the British Black and Tans (used in Ireland). These men often went on to have an important influence on later events and it might well be argued that the inter-war history of Germany, Italy and much of Eastern Europe can be summed up as 'permanent counter-revolution.'

Robert Service
Lenin: Individual and Politics in the October Revolution

Lenin has traditionally been seen as central to events that led to the Bolsheviks coming to power in Russia. Modifying this view, Robert Service still finds that Lenin, despite errors, played a crucial role in the revolution.

By most standards of analysis, Lenin's impact on the Russian Revolution of 1917 was enormous and greater than any other single person's. The story has often been told. At the beginning of April, a month after the abdication of Emperor Nicholas II in the revolution of February and March, he returned by train from Switzerland across Germany and Scandinavia. With his *April Theses* in hand, he persuaded his fellow Bolsheviks not to support the liberal-led Provisional Government of Prince Lvov. At the Bolshevik Party Conference in late April, moreover, his revolutionary strategy was adopted: all power to the soviets of workers', soldiers' and peasants' deputies; a multilateral peace in Europe without indemnities or annexations; land to the peasants; nationalisation of the commanding heights of industry and banking. He had captured the hearts and minds of his party's leaders, activists and rank and file members.

In the remaining months through to October he verbally assaulted the government. In April, Foreign Minister Milyukov reassured his British and French allies that the expansionist war aims of Nicholas II remained the aims of the Provisional Government. Lenin indicated that this confirmed the basis of his own mistrust of the Provisional government. In June, the Provisional Government ordered a re-opening of the offensive on the Eastern front, and Lenin argued that this proved that a policy of mere defence was no longer being followed even though the more socialist parties – the Mensheviks and the Socialist Revolutionaries – had acquired power in the Provisional Government and thus supplied ministers seeking to control the liberals. In July an anti-governmental demonstration in Petrograd was put down by force. Again Lenin queried why the post-Romanov administration found it necessary to fire on its own people. In August, General Kornilov led a right-wing military coup; it was unsuccessful, but the obvious sympathy of most liberal politicians for Kornilov made it more plausible for Lenin to say that the Provisional Government could not be trusted.

Lenin spent the year in intensive action. He had a knack of adopting a style appropriate to modern open politics. He started to wear a workman's cap, now known as a Lenin cap, in order to identify himself with the working class. He became, after initial diffidence and much subsequent effort, an impressive orator. He wrote prolifically for the press, especially for his party newspaper *Pravda*. He assiduously attended and chaired the Central Committee of the Bolshevik Party whenever he could.

In September, furthermore, he judged that the party should seize power. The Petrograd and Moscow Soviets had by then gone over to the Bolsheviks. Other urban soviets in the rest of Russia could be expected to do the same in the near future. Lenin argued that the chance should be grabbed. He feared that the Provisional Government of Aleksandr Kerenski (who took over the premiership from Prince Lvov in July) might take repressive action against the Bolsheviks. He also maintained that the European socialist revolution was imminent. Soon, he asserted, Germany and Britain would possess Red administrations. Thus the Bolshevik-led revolutionary regime in Petrograd would not stand alone. There was still opposition to him among Bolsheviks. At the Central Committee meetings of 10 and 16 October his erstwhile followers, Kamenev and Zinoviev, challenged his analysis. But returning to Petrograd in disguise (with an ill-fitting wig and with his beard shaved off) he faced them down. On 25 October 1917 the insurrection against the Provisional government began. Kerenski's cabinet was overthrown. A new regime was installed. The new government, called the Council of People's Commissars, was to be headed by Vladimir Ilich Lenin.

Reassessing Lenin's role

All this, on the face of things, is a record of unconditional success by a single determined politician. His personal vision and his will to pull his party into line with his ideas was supposedly the crucial factor in the collapse of Aleksandr Kerenski's rule and the accession to power of an uncompromising socialist administration. The October Revolution has often and widely been held to have been predominantly Lenin's revolution.

But was it? Certainly Lenin had a heavier impact on the course of events than anyone else. The point is, however, that great historical processes are wrought not only by individuals. There were other mighty factors at work as well in Russia in 1917. The conditions for a seizure of power with the sanction of exhausted workers, war-weary soldiers and angry peasants could hardly have been more favourable. There was little prospect of Russia's Allies intervening militarily on the side of the Provisional Government; Britain and

France had their hands full on the Western front. In addition, the Provisional Government had tremendous problems of its own. The economy slumped into precipitate decline. Food supplies plummeted as the peasants found little incentive to trade their grain when the industrial goods they wanted were scarcely available. Transport was anyway being disrupted, and such grain as was purchased by the state was conveyed with difficulty to the towns. The army had the priority for food supplies and transport.

The problems affected industry too. Raw material shortages impeded factory production. Moreover, the Provisional Government (like Nicholas II's ministers before it) had to pay for its armaments and grain in paper currency, and the resultant inflation wiped out any gains in the wages of workers. Many firms, especially in 1917, went into liquidation. The working class was fearful lest, in the absence of unemployment relief, it might starve in the forthcoming winter of 1917–1918; the middle class was unhappy because the real value of its dividends was falling.

A people ripe for revolution

Yet the February Revolution of 1917 had unleashed forces that were barely controllable from the start. The emperor Nicholas II had abdicated and handed power to liberals without consulting the country. The Provisional Government lacked the legitimacy of an elected administration. The officials in many ministries, too, were associated with the old regime. Nor could the Provisional Government depend on the normal forces of law and order. The tsarist police had fled for their lives in the February Revolution; its personnel were among the most detested of all the functionaries of Nicholas II. The army was too unsettled to be deployed against the populace in town or village. Most recruits were peasants, and they were as unlikely to support the new regime as their relatives back in the countryside; and, in the early days of the February Revolution, they had taken revenge on notorious disciplinarians in the armed forces (where terms of service were notoriously severe and arbitrary).

For most of the year the Provisional government survived through guile and rhetoric. The guile stemmed from the inclusion of more socialists, Mensheviks and Socialist Revolutionaries, in the cabinet so as to neutralise the feeling that the authorities were out of touch with pro-socialist aspirations among the so-called 'masses'. The rhetoric was evident in the use of the mass media by the most talented orator among the ministers, Aleksandr Kerenski, who eventually became premier. Kerenski's output of posters (and even postcards) to relay his physical image; his brash and emotive speeches; his use of the resources of the Russian cinema: all these marked him out as a man who would have coped adequately with his governmental duties in normal times.

Yet the times were far from being normal, and Lenin's push for an end to the policies of the liberals had advantages from the start. There was a widely-held assumption that the urban middle class was living well while soldiers languished in trenches and workers grew hungrier; and the idea that nothing would change unless a break with the bourgeoisie was undertaken gained ground. It is doubtful that such attitudes were mainly the consequences of Lenin's activities. The extraordinary change in Russian politics in 1917 has to be taken into account. These were not just representative politics with politicians being chosen and sent off to defend the interests of constituencies. There were also participatory politics. Russia became a debating society. An English nurse going out on the Transiberian railway noted that fellow travellers in her carriage even elected a council to organise the food distribution on the train for the length of the journey. Every social group had its own aspirations and set up its own bodies. The most famous were the soviets of the workers and soldiers. Soviet in Russian means 'council'; and every other group, too, had its councils and committees. Sectional politics, with groups competing and bargaining and demanding, were the rule of the day.

This affected even the countryside, where urban political issues were not often talked about or understood. The peasants could easily organise themselves for action. They had their village land communes wherein household elders could get together to discuss local affairs. Freed from the weight of the tsarist administration, the Russian people grasped their freedoms. The police had fled the towns; the land captains had vanished from the villages.

The self-liberating popular movement surged onwards. Strikes and demonstrations brought higher wages to workers. When the factory owners refused to bargain and even shut down firms, the workers stayed inside the gates and kept on working. Take-overs of closed enterprises began in Petrograd. There was typically less radicalism elsewhere. Even so, the soviets were active and influential in all towns and cities. They became shadow administrations, demanding better working and living conditions and cultural facilities. The organs of the Provisional Government proved unable to cope and the soviets assumed greater power. Without permission of the soviets, no initiatives could be taken in towns and cities. Certain soviets declared independence from the rest of the country. In some cases there was a national dimension; the Ukrainian Rada, for example, wanted less Russian interference in Kiev's affairs. Food supplies; transport; army organisation; law and order: these were aspects of daily life for which the premier Kerenski had little power and no answers, and the soviets filled the gap.

Meanwhile the middle class despaired. Most rural landlords no longer lived on their estates: the peasants cultivated nine-tenths of the arable terrain in European Russia even before the February Revolution, but resented the rates they had to pay. They insisted that an immediate and final solution of the land question should be attempted. By this they intended that the Provisional Government should transfer the land to the peasants. As early as March 1917 certain land communes in Penza province had embarked on expropriations.

Industrialists and bankers held on longer in the towns. Efforts were made to persuade the workers that they would achieve nothing by confrontation. A bosses' offensive was launched. But the lockouts enraged the workers further. Stories of war profiteering proliferated, and there was much annoyance that the Provisional government took the side of the owners in cases of industrial conflict. There had always been a chasm between the middle and working classes in Russia. It was wider than in other countries. Many towns were hardly worthy of the name. Ivanovo-Voznesensk, a so-called city which depended entirely on its wealth from textile manufacturing, was akin to a South American shanty-town in housing, sewage and other physical and social amenities. Workers knew they received a poor deal. On the other hand, the middle class was irritated that the conventional ways of bringing the workforce back to heel were unavailable. Workers could no longer be bribed because the economy was collapsing, and they could not be forced because the soviets already held the ultimate authority.

Lenin and the Bolsheviks

Thus Lenin was not the prime instigator of the popular movements for socio-political and economic change in Russia and its subject regions after the February Revolution. Thousands of locally-based and locally-led revolutions occurred, and many of these had taken place before the events of 25 October 1917 in Petrograd.

The Bolshevik Party aimed to take full advantage of this favourable situation. Lenin's assistance was not always helpful. He made a series of gaffes which could have led to disaster for the party. In April he urged a general policy of seizing power, and some party activists in the capital took him at his words – and nearly brought about a full-scale repression against the Bolsheviks. In the same month he enunciated several policies which would have lost the party votes. He talked of the need for European civil war; dictatorship of the proletariat; land nationalisation. None of these ideas appealed widely to the Russian population, and the party central leadership sought to get him to modify his language so that the rising popularity of Bolshevism might be maintained. In June and July 1917 Lenin was remarkably remiss in not stopping street demonstrations which offered the Provisional Government yet further chances of dealing with the Bolsheviks before it was too late.

The greatest woe for the party, however, would have taken place if the Central Committee had obeyed him in September when he urged an instant seizure of power. The Bolsheviks held only a handful of city soviets at the time (admittedly including Petrograd and Moscow). Although Kerenski was weak, he would have been strong enough to suppress the Bolsheviks with the support of his Menshevik and Socialist-Revolutionary allies. The Bolshevik Party would probably have been wiped out in the process. No wonder the Central Committee destroyed his letters.

From all this it is clear that the Bolshevik Party had a life of its own. At the central level there were many skilled politicians. Trotsky, who joined the party in late July, was Lenin's equal as an intellectual, and as an organiser and orator he had the edge; he also had a surer sense of tactical possibilities. Kamenev was an adept advocate in the Petrograd Soviet, and Zinoviev could be relied upon to tour workers' meetings in quest of popular support. Sverdlov was the powerhouse in the Central Committee Secretariat. These leaders were independently-thinking individuals who did not need to be told everything by Lenin. They, too wanted revolution. They, too, had operated for years as revolutionaries and felt that the moment had come to settle scores with the middle class. The Bolshevik Central Committee was not a one-man band. It was a collection of talented organisers, policy-makers and theorists.

And the party as a whole was a dynamic social organism. The rules stated that policy and activity should be determined centrally. But the Bolshevik Party in 1917 was highly anarchic. Local committees did more or less as they pleased. Communications with the Central Committee were frail and intermittent. Decisions were taken locally about vital political issues out of necessity as well as from choice.

This meant that the Bolsheviks could react flexibly and rapidly to specific local requirements. They also lacked the burdens of responsibility that affected their rival parties which had joined the various coalition cabinets of the Provisional Government. It was not only the Bolshevik central leaders who were used to using their initiative. Local leaders had worked in the political underground while Nicholas II had been on the throne. They were practical men and women. They had disliked the pretensions of émigrés like

Lenin before 1917. They knew what they wanted out of the revolution, and they sought to get it. Their efforts to turn Bolsheviks into a mass party were especially successful. By December 1917 there were 200,000–300,000 members. Two thirds of these were said to be workers. The Bolsheviks, unlike their competitors, had a direct line to the feelings of workers. There is evidence that such workers held the party to radical strategical ideas when the central and local party leaders wavered.

Lenin's Revolution

Lenin was lucky to have their support. He was a bundle of great energy. But that energy was finite. Its deployability, too, was finite. Let us look at the limits on his possible impact. A number of factors are usually left out of the reckoning. For most of the eight months between the February and October Revolutions Lenin was not in Russia. He returned from Switzerland in early April, and was forced to flee to Finland in early July. He came back to Petrograd only in early October. In such circumstances, when attention to the details of swiftly changing politics was essential, Lenin simply could not have done or even co-ordinated everything.

Furthermore, Lenin visited no city in Russia in 1917 apart from Petrograd. The pictures and posters of him which are so familiar to us were reproduced in their millions only after the October Revolution. *Pravda* had no photographs, and the Russian movie-newsreels contained no footage of him but concentrated instead on Kerenski. Of course, Lenin wrote a good deal, almost always for *Pravda*. But *Pravda* had a circulation of only 80,000–100,000 at its peak: not very much for a population of around 130 million. It must also be borne in mind that nearly half the copies of *Pravda* were sold in Petrograd, and that this left few indeed for the rest of the country. The idea that Lenin's views on each and every latest political development were regularly and carefully discussed by all the citizens of the former Russian empire is an absurdity.

And yet the challenge to the older conventional wisdom can be pressed too far. The notion that the October socialist revolution came wholly or nearly wholly from below is overstated. The revolution from above, initiated by Lenin in the Central Committee of mid-October and carried through on 25 October, still had a crucial impact. It was not the only impact, but it had vast importance nevertheless.

The starting point of analysis should be that there would probably have been a socialist regime in place in Russia by the end of the year whether or not Lenin had existed. Kerenski was a broken reed, and the threat of a Bolshevik action was already by autumn provoking the left wings of the more moderate socialist parties to demand a transfer of power to an exclusively socialist administration. Both the collapse of the economy and the yearning for peace had compelled a total reconsideration of strategy. This helps to explain Lenin's sense of urgency. He himself, unlike many (and probably most) Bolsheviks, did not want a coalition with other parties. He talked of the imminence of political counterrevolution in Russia; but he must have known that Kerenski's days were numbered.

Thus Lenin made a difference after all. The timing of the collapse of the Provisional Government was more his work than the consequence of the socio-political environment, or of the actions of the soviets, or of the expressed wish of the Bolshevik Party as a whole. Lenin's insistence on putting the seizure of power on the agenda was strong, and Trotsky was probably right in stating that no one else could have put the item there in mid-October.

The obvious decisive result was that he had a great influence over the personal composition and policies of the new socialist government. Neither he nor Trotsky wanted a coalition with the more moderate socialist parties. Lenin had been devious. Despite hints of this intention, he had never spelled them out in advance and no Bolshevik had had the sense to interrogate him. Nonetheless it remains hard to imagine how a coalition of all socialist parties in 1917 would have long endured. The mutual hostilities of the Bolsheviks and the anti-Bolsheviks were robust. Even if a coalition government had been formed, Lenin was a past master of disruption and would have constantly found reasons to question the sense and integrity of his coalition partners. He felt himself to be a man of destiny. He was not personally vain. But he had a high tacit estimate of his own capacities, and assumed that everything would go to the dogs unless he was in charge of his party and his government.

His strategy for socialist revolution was deeply flawed. There was no European socialist revolution. This was a vital failure from the standpoint of Lenin's plans. It meant that the new Soviet republic would not be bordered by fraternal socialist states. Instead the Bolsheviks and their fledgeling state would have to endure a lengthy epoch of political besiegement and economic pressure from Western capitalist powers.

The ramifications at home were equally dire. The Bolsheviks had taken it for granted that the First World War would quickly end and that the factories could be transferred to production for the civilian economy. They predicted that this would induce the peasants to trade their grain freely again. Food supplies to the towns would thereby be restored. But peace did not immediately break out in

Europe. Nor did the opponents of the Bolsheviks in Russia give up the struggle against them. In the Constituent Assembly elections held in late 1917, the Bolsheviks polled less than a quarter of the votes. They did well among the working class in the towns, but the bulk of the electorate refused to back them. The lurch into authoritarianism had never been unlikely for a party leadership which had always proclaimed the virtues of a dictatorship of the proletariat. The chances became stronger within months of the October Revolution. In December 1917 the Cheka was established, and the shootings of worker demonstrators against the Bolsheviks occurred in the winter of 1917–1918. Forcible requisitioning of grain, too, occurred in ensuing months.

This is not to deny the idealism which infused the first large-scale attempt at socialist revolution. Leading Bolsheviks sincerely believed that they lived at the dawn of the era of global socialism; they thought that their revolution would eradicate political oppression, national enmity and economic exploitation. Lenin may have tricked others; but he also tricked himself. He was not the devil incarnate. He genuinely adhered to at least some ideals which even non-socialists can see as having been designed to benefit the mass of humanity.

Robert Service is Reader in Soviet History and Politics at the School of Slavonic and East European Studies, London.

Chris Wrigley
The Impact of the Russian Revolution of October 1917 in Europe 1917–20

The October Revolution in Russia was a consequence of the upheavals of the First World War. In turn it was to add to the pressures for substantial change that were exerted on other central and eastern European countries during the latter part of the war and its aftermath. Its example encouraged the revolutionary Left, made clear the divisions between revolutionary and democratic socialists and provided the forces of Order throughout Europe with a dangerous enemy against whom they could unite in the cause of counter-revolution.

Military defeat and the appeal of peace

The Bolshevik Revolution's impact was considerable. Yet it should not be exaggerated. The wartime pressures which brought about the February and October 1917 Revolutions in Russia were present in the German, Habsburg and Ottoman empires which also collapsed in defeat. There were strong forces at work before 1914 which might have undermined these régimes in time. However, the First World War was decisive in bringing these empires down. The Tsarist régime in Russia faced major problems in 1914, notably a serious strike wave. Yet, the weight of historical opinion now suggests that Russia was not then on the verge of revolution. Similarly, though the Habsurg Monarchy continued to face major nationality probelms, it took the substantial stresses of the war and military defeat to demolish it. As for the German Kaiserreich, though faced with a Socialist Party (the SPD) which was the largest party in the Reichstag from 1912, it was not remotely in danger of being overthrown in 1914.

Defeat, along with wartime social hardship, discredited the ruling élites of central and eastern Europe. The failure to ensure ample supplies of the necessities of life along with military defeat undermined allegiance to régimes which had never fully asked their people for democratic support. In Russia many of such powers as the Duma had enjoyed in 1906 had been whittled away by 1914. In Germany, while working men could vote for the SPD until defeat was looming in the autumn of 1918 the SPD was excluded from office. Defeat shook the Central Powers and their allies but nowhere was it more of a shock than Germany where, until beyond the summer of 1918, the German army was believed to be invincible.

Revolution in 1917–19 was also linked to peace. In Russia many had hoped that the February Revolution would be followed by an end to the war, be it in victory or a compromise peace. With the failure of the Kerenski offensive in the summer of 1917 the pro-war politicians' rhetoric of victory appeared empty, while the social deprivation which had helped bring about the February Revolution continued to worsen. Lenin's promise of peace had a powerful appeal. In Germany the removal of the Kaiser was a prerequisite for negotiating peace terms with President Wilson, Lloyd George and Clemenceau. In contrast, in Hungary, the expected loss of territory as a result of defeat made a major contribution to the collapse of the liberal democratic government of Count Michael Karolyi. This brought the creation of the Hungarian Soviet Republic on 21 March 1919 and in turn, under its wing, the proclamation in Kosice of the Slovakian Soviet Republic in June 1919.

The role of soldiers and sailors

The role of soldiers and sailors was often decisive in determining the success or failure of revolution and counter-revolution. Frequently it was garrison troops who played the key role. They experienced similar privations as the nearby civilian population and they were often in contact with dissident views. The civil unrest in Petrograd in February 1917 took on a very serious aspect when the soldiers in the garrisons declined to act against the demonstrators and then joined them. In contrast, in 1905, the armed forces in Petrograd and Moscow had remained loyal to the Tsar and had taken ruthless action against working-class dissidents. In the autumn of 1917 Russian sailors in Petrograd and Kronstadt were key Bolshevik supporters.

Revolution in Germany began when sailors of the High Sea Fleet mutinied in October 1918 after being given orders to sail for a suicidal final battle with the Royal Navy. In so doing they ended any chance that a 'revolution from above' (the existing ruling élite's attempts to establish a constituional monarchy) would assuage popular unrest and instead took Germany into a 'revolution from below'. Unrest spread fast from Kiel and other coastal towns, with the emergence of sailors' councils there being followed by the springing up across Germany of soldiers' and workers' councils. However, once the war was over the most radical soldiers and sailors were eager to return to civilian life, thus ending the strength of the council movement in the armed forces and leaving the army to return to its traditional role in Germany as a bulwark of Order.

However, during the period of mobilisation the nature of European armed forces was changed. By the time of the October 1917 Revolution some 15.3 million men had been called up out of a total Russian population of some 139.3 million. The figures were also huge for the other main European belligerents. By the end of the war Germany had enlisted some 11.1 million, Austria 7.8 million, France 8.3 million, Britain 5.7 million and Italy 5 million. For many of these men it was an unwelcome experience. In Russia, and many other countries, dissident factory workers were often drafted into the armed forces. Many skilled German workers were forced to join the High Seas Fleet. Across Europe millions of men who had previously moved only a few miles from their home town were taken to distant battle zones. Peasants, who resented being uprooted from their village, mixed with urban workers, many of whom were radical. Reluctant soldiers and sailors were often amenable to arguments which would end their unwanted service, whether these arguments were made by Bolsheviks or others. Thousands indicated their views by deserting. All armies experienced this – but it was carried out on a great scale in the Russian and Austrian-Hungarian armies. Such armies as Kornilov's marching on Petrograd in July 1917 or parts of the German returning defeated to the Fatherland in autumn 1918, just melted away.

With the end of the war in most countries there was widespread fear of the demobilised soldiers, especially if they were unemployed. In Britain, the government had strong doubts, in 1919, as to the dependability of soldiers if they were used to break strikes. Fears were also expressed that working class protesters, many of them veterans of the Western Front, would be better trained than the troops sent to quell them. Yet there were former soldiers in all countries who were eager to use their military skills against the Left and nationalists. These joined the *Freikorps* in Germany, the Whites in Russia and eastern Europe and the Black and Tans and auxiliaries for service in Ireland.

Shortages of Food and Fuel

Urban industrial areas which experienced high inflation and severe shortages of food and fuel were especially susceptible to revolution in 1918–19. This had been the case in Petrograd which suffered badly in the winter of 1916–7, with half of the estimated 25 per cent drop in real wages between 1913 and the February Revolution taking place then. Inflation accelerated in urban Russia between the February and October Revolutions. Similarly in Germany and Austria-Hungary, apart from some skilled workers in essential industries, most wage earners had a hard time as food and fuel became scarce. In Germany, in spite of government controls on rents, prices and wages, the retail price index more than doubled betwen 1913 and 1918. In addition to the common wartime dislocation of domestic food supplies (through withdrawal of manpower, limited supplies of machinery and fertilisers as well as military damage), the Central Powers suffered severely from the Allied Blockade which was maintained until the terms of peace were agreed in mid-1919.

Shortages of food and fuel did much to radicalise workers across Europe. Unfair distribution of what was available caused considerable indignation. Goods which were not on sale in ordinary shops were available on the black market or in expensive restaurants. Food queues across Europe became radical forums. Before the February 1917 Revolution in Russia the Petrograd secret policy warned that 'the queues had the same force as revolutionary meetings and tens of thousands of revolutionary leaflets'. The comment made by the commissioners investigating the causes of industrial unrest in 1917 in Scotland could easily have been made elsewhere in Europe: 'The actual increase in the cost of living does not appear to be so important a factor in the workers' mind as the belief that profittering exists'. Across urban Europe popular sentiment declared in favour of a 'moral economy', with 'fair shares' and equality of treatment, rather than one led by market forces.

Urban industrial workers and the war

Industrial workers in large urban areas were the group most involved in revolutionary activity in 1917–20. The war both strengthened their bargaining position and accentuated their grievances.

The massive withdrawal of manpower into the armed forces put skilled labour in essential war industries at a premium. In Britain, for instance, during the first year of the war there were reductions of between 16 and 24 per cent in the total number of males working in coal, iron and steel, engineering, shipbuilding, electrical engineering and chemicals. The need for massive increases in output in a 'war of production' ensured that governments had to take greater heed of organised labour than in the past. In Britain, Germany and elsewhere the state pressed employers into recognising the unions. Joint employer-employee boards were set up and concessions made on wages and welfare.

Yet the rapid expansion of war industries created major tensions both outside and inside the workplace. Conditions in industrial areas across Europe had been bad before 1914. The influx of munitions workers made them even worse. Between 1911 and 1921 the population of Milan expanded from 600,000 to 718,000 and Turin from 427,000 to 518,000. The numbers employed at major plants across Europe mushroomed. At Woolwich Arsenal, London, the workforce rose from 10,868 at the outbreak of the war to a peak of 74,467 in May 1917. In Turin, Fiat's workforce expanded from 3,500 to 40,000. In such circumstances there was acute overcrowding and, as demand shot past supply and rents soared, rioting took place.

Employment was strongly skewed towards war work. In Britain, the numbers in civil employment fell from 19,440,000 in 1914 to 17,060,000 in 1918, while the numbers employed in the metal trades rose by 34 per cent, from 1,804,000 (9.4 per cent of whom were female) in July 1914 to 2,418,000 (24.6 per cent female) in July 1918. In Petrograd, the number of workers in metallurgical trades nearly doubled from 150,043 in 1913 to 291,356 in early 1917. In Germany, the number of workers employed in industries meeting military needs (metals, chemicals, petroleum and electrical) rose from 2,116,000 to 3,050,000 between 1913 and 1918.

Such rapid expansion led to much industrial strife. Much unrest was caused by the arrival of unskilled female and male labour to do work hitherto the preserve of men who had served apprenticeships or served their time learning on the job. Similarly in Britain, Italy and elsewhere there were clashes as employers accelerated major changes that were already underway in engineering. Further friction was caused where there was state regulation which laid down financial and even custodial penalties for industrial misdemeanours such as bad timekeeping. So across Europe skilled workers frequently were in the vanguard of industrial unrest as they tried to defend the work patterns to which they were accustomed. In opposing many of these workshop changes socialist shop stewards found a common cause with the more conservative of their workmates.

Growing state intervention placed the state in the industrial firing line. Where there was state control of industry, strikes became directed at the state even when the grievances could be categorised as 'industrial'. However, a feature of the war was the politicisation of strikes. In Berlin from 1916 onwards, for example, shop stewards made not just economic demands but others such as the freeing of the socialist Karl Liebknecht from gaol, the lifting of martial law, the ending of the three-class discriminatory electoral system in Prussia and peace.

The impact of the Bolshevik Revolution on the Left

The Bolshevik Revolution in Russia was a response to the continuing turmoil and despair of the First World War and an encouragement to revolutionary socialists facing similar circumstances elsewhere. It made real half a century's talk of socialists and workers running a state. The Bolsheviks took the citadels of power in Russia and held on to them for some seventy years. Hence the October Revolution's main impact was as an example to emulate or a warning of what could occur in other states.

Emulation proved difficult even in the Europe of 1917–20. Bolshevik survival in Russia was due to special circumstances. Russia was huge, the Whites were divided and so draconian in their behaviour in reconquered areas that they alienated much potential support. Also the Allies were sufficiently war-weary not to be willing or politically able to assign large resources to further warfare on a large scale. While the Russian peasants were far from enthusiastic about the Bolsheviks, they wanted to hold on to the land and saw the Whites as a greater evil. They would restore the land to the former landlords and butcher those who had been involved in its seizure. Moreover, Lenin was single-mindedly determined to hold on to power and Trotsky succeeded in forging the Red Army into an effective fighting force.

Elsewhere soviet republics did not last long. In the case of Hungary the Allied Powers could crush Bela Kun's regime without great expense. Romania and Czechoslovakia had territorial interests in the old Hungarian lands and the former readily sent an army into Budapest. In Hungary the poorer peasants supported the urban revolutionaries while they promised land redistribution, but lost interest when that did not occur.

In Germany, the Bavarian and other socialist or soviet republics were soon put down by the army and the *Freikorps*. The red uprisings were uncoordinated and so could be suppressed one by one. In spite of the October Revolution, and all that had happened in Germany in late 1918, the German revolutionary Left was ill-prepared for revolution. Its leaders, unlike Lenin, expected revolution sponteanously to occur with little need for organisation. Moreover, though there was a large urban working class compared with Russia, there was also a strong and determined middle class and, outside of Bavaria, a conservative peasantry.

Yet if the spread of communist states in Europe was to await the upheavals of another world war and the arrival of a powerful Red Army the October Revolution nevertheless played a major role in transforming the politics of the Left and Right in Europe. Both the democratic and the revolutionary Left had enhanced appeal during the turmoil of 1914–19, during which period collectivist and egalitarian ideas were boosted by the increased role of the state and by the limited supplies of food and fuel. The success of Lenin and the Bolsheviks added considerable credibility and prestige to revolutionary socialists. This was especially so early on when the Bolsheviks were revealing the acquisitive war aims of the Allies (by publishing secret treaties) and were trying to implement a peace of no annexations and indemnities at Brest-Litovsk. It continued to be so during the period of Allied intervention but diminished once the Bolsheviks' suppression of the Mensheviks and Socialist Revolutionaries became widely known.

In giving Lenin and the Bolsheviks immense prestige, the October Revolution further deepened the divisions in socialism. These were well established in the late nineteenth century and reinforced before the First World War. The war accentuated them further, with European labour dividing between pro-war and anti-war groups. In Germany, the most notable example, the mighty SPD which had contained a range of disparate views before 1914, split with a sizeable minority forming the ISPD (Independent Social Democratic Party) in April 1917. After the Bolshevik Revolution many Marxists broke away from social democratic parties to form communist parties. These were set up in Germany and Hungary in late 1918, in Britain and France in 1920 and in Italy and Czechoslovakia in 1921. Lenin formalised and underlined the divisions by creating the Third (or Communist) International in March 1919. From its Second Congress, in the summer of 1920, it set its Twenty-One Conditions of Admission which divided the sheep from the goats, the unblemished revolutionaries from unregenerate democratic socialists.

Europe's leading democratic socialists, for the most part, soon lost any enthusiasm they had ever had for Lenin and the Bolsheviks. Figures such as Arthur Henderson (Parliamentary leader of the British Labour Party 1908–10, 1914–17 and 1931–32) never had any in the first place. He had supported Kerenski and condemned the Bolsheviks *before* the October Revolution. He continued to do so afterwards, even arranging for Kerenski to speak twice at the Labour Party Conference in June 1918. In Germany, Friedrich Ebert made clear his attitude towards revolution: 'I don't want it; I hate it like sin'. He and his socialist colleagues in office used the army and the *Freikorps* to suppress the revolutionary Left. British Labour and other moderate socialists revived the old Second International as a forum for democratic socialists. This was sufficiently anti-Bolshevik for some left-wing, but not revolutionary, socialists to form a third international body, the Vienna Union – dubbed 'the two-and-a-half International' – which for several years existed at a midway position between the Second and Third Internationals.

Thus the October Revolution contributed to the fragmentation of international socialism, a process underway from the outset of the First World War.

The impact of the Bolshevik Revolution on the Right

In the eyes of the Right the Bolshevik Revolution gave body to the spectre that Marx and Engels had conjured up in *The Communist Manifesto* (1848) and which had experienced a brief life in 1871 in the Paris Commune. Centre and Right-wing politicians across Europe mobilised the votes of those with property, however meagre, by warning of 'the Bolshevik peril'.

In central Europe counter-revolutionary forces were often mustered with speed. These drew on the old officer élites, landowners, peasants, the middle class and the unorganised working class. In Germany *Freikorps*, led by officers and funded by big business, gained large numbers of men in a week or two at the turn of 1918–19. In Hungary, in 1919, Admiral Horthy rapidly recruited a counter-revolutionary army with the eager encouragement of the British authorities and the acquiescence of the French. In the Austrian provinces the rural Right drew on arms brought back from the Italian front. In Italy the seizure of Fiume by Gabriele D'Annunzio and a band of irregular troops revived memories of Garibaldi and boosted the fascist and nationalist squads which terrorised labour movement activists in many regions.

Fear of Bolshevism helped accelerate the move of businessmen and the middle class towards the Right, be it to the democratic Right, such as the Conservatives in Britain, or to extreme Right leaders ranging from the authoritarian Horthy in Hungary to Mussolini and later to Hitler. The long anticipated Red Revolution in Germany did not follow that in Russia. Indeed the upheavals of 1918–20 helped to weaken moderate socialism in Germany. Far from moving to the Left, as seemed likely in 1918–20, Germany, Austria, Hungary and Italy moved to the Right after 1919.

Further Reading

Acton, Edward *Rethinking the Russian Revolution* (Arnold, 1989).

Carsten, F. L. *Revolution In Central Europe 1918–19* (Maurice Temple Smith 1972, reprinted Wildwood House, 1988).

Dukes, Paul *October and the World: Perspectives on the Russian Revolution* (Macmillan, 1979).

Geary, Dick *European Labour Politics from 1900 to the Depression* (Macmillan, 1991).

Lindemann, A. S. *The 'Red Years': European Socialism Versus Bolshevism 1919–1921* (University of California Press, 1974).

Lyttelton, A. *The Seizure of Power: Fascism in Italy 1919–1929* (Princeton University Press, 1973, second edition, 1987).

Magraw, Roger *A History of the French Working Class*, Vol. 2. (Blackwell, 1992).

Wrigley, Chris (ed.) *Challenges of Labour: Central and Western Europe 1917–1920* (Routledge, 1993).

Chris Wrigley is Professor of Modern British History at Nottingham University.

PART III
Europe of the Dictators

It is easy to present European history between the two world wars as just a struggle between dictatorship and democracy. Such an interpretation misses two facts. Firstly, the division between dictatorship and democracy was not always clear. Dictators worked within democracy when it suited them. Hitler came to power through elections rather than naked force, and Mussolini governed along with democratic parties for a number of years before instituting a full dictatorship. Marshal Pétain was granted dictatorial powers of France in 1940 by an overwhelming vote of the same parliament that had voted for the Popular Front four years earlier. Furthermore, 'democratic' politicians often resorted to undemocratic means. Brüning governed by decree law during the late Weimar Republic as did Daladier during the last years of the French Third Republic. Secondly, there were enormous differences between the dictators. The most obvious of these distinguished the dictatorship of Lenin and Stalin in Russia from those in the rest of Europe. During the Cold War some historians suggested that both these kinds of dictatorship could be grouped under the heading of 'totalitarian'. However, in recent years, historians have argued that not even Stalin or Hitler exercised total power, and have laid increasing stress on the class relations that distinguished the Soviet state from other dictatorships. Hitler, Mussolini, Pétain and Franco all challenged the free market economy, attacked particular business interests and made claims to social radicalism, but none of them ever mounted a systematic assault on capitalism or the existing ownership of property.

A more serious distinction is that between fascists and conservatives. Fascists claimed to be hostile to the very institutions (such as the Church, the army and the landed aristocracy) that mattered most to conservatives, and, though fascists often did little practical damage to these institutions once in power, they remained more aggressive and radical in tone than their conservative allies. Fascists tended to subordinate all institutions to the authority of a single party and they placed great faith in a single charismatic leader. However, these differences did not prevent fascists and conservative dictators from co-operating. Hitler and Mussolini helped General Franco in Spain and tolerated Marshal Pétain in France. Furthermore, divisions within a single country might be blurred.

Franco built his power on the army and the Church, but he also took over an existing fascist organisation (the Falange) and made it a central instrument of his new state.

Even within regimes and movements that are normally labelled 'fascist' there are many contradictions, and almost no general rule can be devised without an exception coming to mind. Fascism in Italy and Germany was nurtured by defeat or disappointment in the First World War, but the Rumanian Iron Guard arose in a nation that had enlarged its frontiers by a factor of five in the aftermath of the First World War. Fascism in Germany emphasised loyalty to the race and looked back to a mythologised past; fascism in Italy emphasised loyalty to the state (anti-semitic legislation was only introduced in Italy in 1938) and glorified technological modernity.

Most importantly, no dictatorship (whether communist, conservative, or fascist) can be separated from the local context in which it operated. For all their rhetoric about power, every dictator depended on his capacity to obtain the co-operation of a section of the people under his rule. Stalin's power in Smolensk was mediated by local party officials who used collectivisation and purges to settle scores of their own; Hitler's power in Bavaria was seen through a prism of Catholic conservatism; Mussolini's power in the Italian south depended on notables who continued to regard the state as a source of money and employment for their clients. No dictator succeeded in abolishing politics.

Roderick Gordon
Mussolini 1919–22:
The Rise to Power

Post-war liberal Italy was the sufferer of many illnesses, some real, others imaginary. However, because of the emergence of right-wing propagandists such as Gabriele D'Annunzio and Benito Mussolini, it became impossible to distinguish between the two. This was a significant factor in the successful and brutal rise to power of Mussolini.

Italy in 1919 was the victim of a series of overlapping social and economic problems which had been exacerbated by, or were the result of, the war. In 1914 there had been 5 lire to the dollar, now there were 28; the cost of living since 1914 had risen by 560%, and unemployment stood at 1,122,000. Italian industry was paralysed by a rash of strikes in 1919–20, known to history as the *Bienno Rosso* when socialist-organised strikes and 'occupation of the factories' led to a loss of 53 million working days. In the countryside the peasants were encouraged by the socialists to take land from the *latifundios* (the large landowners). This high level of disruption made it unexpectedly easy for Mussolini to bind together the different classes in Italian society by conjuring the imaginary spectre of Bolshevik Revolution (in reality the socialists were too inert and divided to make such a thing possible) and create support for Fascism.

The Versailles treaty also created a *malada imaginaria* in the question of Fiume which, though containing substantial numbers of Italians, was situated in a hinterland composed almost entirely of Croats. Under the terms of the treaty, this city on the Adriatic coast was awarded to Yugoslavia. However, in September 1919, in a daring attack led by the one-eyed poet and novelist, Gabriele D'Annunzio, accompanied by a private army of 'legionaries', the prototype of the fascist *squadristi*, Fiume was captured for Italy. This affair was viewed by the majority of Italians as an act of dazzling nationalist heroism, which reflected badly on the timid policy of the liberal government who had accepted the loss of Fiume.

At this time, D'Annunzio was a much more famous figure on the nationalist right than Mussolini, and it was he who was to give fascism much of its distinctive style and many of its (largely spurious) ideas. This included the concept of a 'March on Rome', the dressing of his followers in black shirts, the use of castor oil on opponents, the necessity for a political movement to have its own paramilitary force, the demagogic style of speaking from the balcony, the song *Giovenezza*, (later to be sung by the *squadristi*), the Roman salute, the idea of the Mediterranean as *Mare Nostrum* (Our Sea), the Corporate State and the use of violence and propaganda (to discredit opponents and to disguise the meaning and intention of fascism, so that its support would be as wide as possible). While stealing D'Annunzio's ideas, Mussolini accorded him enormous respect and effectively won his acquiescent support by gifts of money and property, which were deeply appreciated by the poet who was always in debt. The appearance of D'Annunzio on the political scene in 1919 and 1920, was a vital first stage in the evolution of fascism.

Between 1919 and 1922 there were five liberal governments (Orlando, Nitti, Giolitti, Bonomi and Facta). None of these administrations proved capable of finding solutions to the problems besetting Italy: industrial and rural unrest; fascist violence; unemployment; inflation; and nationalist grievances. In relation to the first two, Giolitti in particular, adopted a policy of non-intervention, based on the dangerous philosophy that the less action by the government the less inflammatory the situation would become; the main consequence was to create a fatal impression of weakness. This appeared in great contrast to the strong, dynamic government which appeared to be offered by Benito Mussolini.

Appearance of Mussolini

Mussolini was a journalist and ex-socialist, who had been prominent in the intervention crisis of 1915. During the war he had served on the Isonzo Front and after being injured in an exercise involving a grenade launcher ('the most beautiful moment of my life', he is reported to have said, according to fascist mythology), he returned to journalism in 1917 as Editor of *Il Italia Popolo* at the age of 34. On 23 March 1919, he founded the *Fascio di Combattimento* in Milan, an event which was attended by 118 people, known forever afterwards as the *sansepolcrista* (the number mysteriously doubling and trebling over the years as careerists sought to claim evidence of a prescient commitment to early fascism).

The first fascist programme was indistinguishable from that of the socialists, including demands for an 8-hour day, workers' control in the factories and the rejection of imperialism. In the November elections the fascists only won 2% of the votes, causing the Milanese socialists to stage a mock funeral past Mussolini's house. However, faced with such abysmal lack of success, Mussolini more or less discarded the whole programme and progressively embraced big business, the church, the landowners and the monarchy, while holding out carrots to the working classes with much talk of syndicalism and the corporate state (i.e. where employers and workers' unions would govern the country).

Matters developed in his favour in 1920 when the Fascists began to intervene as strike-breakers and defenders of blackleg labour during the *Bienno Rosso*. Even more important was a tremendous surge in fascism's popularity in north and central rural Italy, particularly the Po Valley and Tuscany. The activities of the socialists and the Catholic peasant unions in attempting redistribution of land in the countryside, had antagonised wide sections of rural society, including not simply the *latifundios*, but also the larger peasant proprietors. Using bases in Bologna, Ferrara and Florence, the Fascist *Ras* (an Ethiopian word meaning 'provincial boss') began to organise gangs of hooligans (known as *squadristi*) to attack the socialists. Prominent amongst the *Ras* were Italo Balbo, Alfredo Arpinati, Robert Farinacci and Dino Grandi, who were virtually independent of Mussolini's control. Under the benevolent gaze of the local police, the squads used a variety of offensive weapons (guns, knives and the forced administration of castor oil) upon socialists and unionists. Between 1920 and 1922 the organisational structure of these movements in the countryside was virtually destroyed. The squads were useful to Mussolini in intimidating opposition, and in gaining the support of big business and the landowners. He added to his status by appearing to be able to control the violence of the squads (apparently responsible for 3,000 deaths between 1920 and 1922), while at the same time he escaped contamination by being too closely associated with them. But he had to be very skilful in preventing the squads and more particularly, the *Ras*, becoming a danger to him.

Widening of support for fascism

During this time fascism had acquired many prominent supporters, including the conductor, Arturo Toscanini (though he soon became disillusioned) and the Futurist painter, Filippo Marinetti. D'Annunzio gave his blessing from occupied Fiume, as did Puccini and the philosopher Benedetto Croce (who was later to become a bitter enemy of Mussolini). Many prominent industrialists had, by 1921, given their support for fascism, including Pirelli, Giovanni Agnelli, the arms manufacturer Ansaldo and the Italian Banking Association. They provided vital financial assistance along with the *latifundios* and ensured the survival of the movement. By 1921, 13% of all students had joined the Fascist Party, as had 32,000 landowners, 24,000 tradesmen, and 14,000 professional people, though the largest numbers were from the peasantry and industrial workers.

The Fascists of the First Hour had been mainly veterans of the war, officers and NCOs, who were to constitute the backbone of the *squadristi*, along with local policemen.

The church, under Pius XI, officially supported the Popolari Party, led by Don Sturzo, which had been formed in 1919. But they began to realise that, despite Mussolini's professed atheism and the youthful novel which he had written entitled *The Cardinal's Mistress*, he was liable to be a much more effective defender of the church against potential expropriation by the socialists. In his speeches Mussolini promised to heal the division between church and state and, in 1922, Pius XI withdrew his sponsorship of the Popolari Party and officially backed the Fascists, advising all Catholics to do the same.

The monarch, Victor Emmanuel, was not particularly sympathetic but his mother, Margherita, was an ardent fascist and he began to be won over, as Mussolini discarded his republicanism and made his famous speech accepting the monarchy on 20 September 1922 at Udine. It was a tradition of the Italian political system that troublesome, radical elements should be absorbed into the government, the process called *transformismo*, and it was widely accepted by 1922 that Mussolini would eventually be given a share in power, a view held by Giolitti, who had entered into a Parliamentary pact with Mussolini in 1921.

Another factor in assisting Mussolini's rise was the pathetic failure of the opposition parties to unite against him. At no time did the Popolari and the socialists appear to realise the threat they were under and they made no attempt to cooperate. They completely failed to counter the inexorable violence of the squads in the towns and the countryside, the socialists exacerbating their weakness further, by splitting into socialist and communist wings as a result of the Livorno conference in January 1921. In August 1922, they finally discredited their movement by an ill-organised general strike whose defeat became known as 'the Caporetto of Italian socialism' (a reference to the Italians' disastrous defeat in 1917). Throughout 1921 and 1922, the *Ras* and the *squadristi* fought their way to power in the provinces and the big cities such as Milan and Bologna, though they had little success in the south.

The March on Rome

In late October 1922 it was decided to implement D'Annunzio's concept of a 'March on Rome'. Mussolini claimed that he was the inspiration behind this plan, but Italo Balbo, in his memoirs, counter-claimed that Mussolini vacillated and had to be prodded by the *Ras*. It was intended that 20–30,000 blackshirts, who were based at Civitavecchia, Tivoli and Monterotondo, would converge upon

Rome and through a mere show of strength cause the government to collapse and hand it over to the fascists.

The Facta government, if it had acted decisively and been supported by Victor Emmanuel, would have had little difficulty in preventing a takeover by the blackshirts, who were poorly armed. However, at the crucial moment on the night of 27–28 October the frayed nerves of Victor Emmanuel, Prime Minister Facta and the Commandant of the Roman military garrison, allowed a situation to develop, whereby against all the apparent odds, Mussolini was able to gain power. At 2.00 a.m. on 28 October 1922, the king accepted the government's request to impose martial law, but by 9.00 a.m. he refused to sign the decree because he had no faith in Facta and had been led to believe that the military garrison could not be relied on to fight the fascists. The king was advised by Salandra, an ex-Premier, to appoint Mussolini Prime Minister, which he did on 29 October 1922. Mussolini was summoned from Milan and installed in office on 30 October.

Conclusion

Mussolini came to power because of Italian liberalism's inability to adjust to the age of mass politics, which as a result of the electoral laws of 1912 and 1919, produced a massive electorate with easily transferable loyalties. Italy itself was weakened by a succession of crises – the intervention debate of 1915, the frustrating experience of war, its humiliation at Versailles, the industrial and rural unrest, the 'spectre of Bolshevism', a multiplying series of economic problems, a weak political system, enfeebled governments who followed outdated policies of non-intervention and *transformismo*. Fascism gathered support because of the weakness of liberalism, the bankruptcy of orthodox conservatism, and the dangers apparent to the middle and upper classes from socialism. Its success was assured because of the tacit approval of the armed forces and the police, combined with Mussolini's opportunistic preparedness to discard ideology and enter into his legendary compact with big business, the landowners, the church and the monarchy. This despite having been a socialist, a peasant, an atheist and a Republican. Mussolini was the one man capable of containing fascism's 'chaos of contradictions', and of creating a movement which could appeal to all classes and prepare the way for the final bluff into power. An important final point to remember is made by F. L. Carsten: 'Without dynamism and ruthlessness it could never have succeeded, however favourable the objective conditions of the post-war years were to its quick development.'

Roderick Gordon is History Tutor at Davies College, Bloomsbury.

Patrick Salmon
The Weimar Republic:
Could it have Survived?

The Weimar Republic should not be seen simply as a doomed interlude between imperial and Nazi Germany. Patrick Salmon explains the severe problems that it faced and the reasons for its eventual collapse.

Although the Weimar Republic collapsed nearly 60 years ago, it is important to remember that Germany in the 1920s was a modern society in some ways very like our own. People listened to the radio, went to dance halls and the cinema, had motor cars. In other words, they led normal lives. The strengths and weaknesses of Weimar society are in many ways similar to the strengths and weaknesses of our own.

It is all too easy to see Weimar in apocalyptic terms as merely a prelude to Nazism – an interlude between imperial and Nazi Germany – rather than in its own right. The republic in fact lasted for 14 eventful years; years of crises of all kinds, in the political, economic, social and cultural spheres. From 1919 to 1923 the Weimar Republic seemed at several times to be on the verge of collapse. It was again in deep crisis after the onset of the Great Depression in 1929. Even the so-called 'golden years' of 1925–29 were highly problematical.

Given this endemic atmosphere of crisis, together with the trauma of defeat in the First World War and Germany's anti-democratic traditions, it is all too easy to write the Weimar Republic off as an unsuccessful experiment in democracy. Before doing so, however, it is necessary to ask three questions. First, was the Weimar Republic doomed from the outset, even if there had been no economic crash in 1929? Secondly, did the crash spell the end, or could the republic still have been rescued? Finally, if the republic *was* doomed, was Nazism the inevitable replacement? Did it have to end in the worst possible form of totalitarian dictatorship?

The legacy of Imperial Germany

No government exists in a historical vacuum, and the Weimar Republic had to live with its legacy from Imperial Germany. In a sense Germany was already in crisis in 1914. The empire created by Bismarck had come into existence only in 1871. Unlike Britain or France, which had existed as unified states for centuries, Germany had only a short history as a nation state. It had been brought together by Prussian military power and by the exclusion of Austria, a solution of the German question which created as many problems as it solved.

Pre-war Germany was also undergoing a process of extremely rapid industrialisation, becoming one of the three leading industrial powers in the world, alongside Britain and the United States, by 1914. Industrialisation sowed the seeds of social tensions, through the urban growth and industrial conflicts it brought in its train. An industrial working class grew up, its interests represented mainly by the Social Democratic Party. By 1912 the SPD had become the largest party in the Reichstag, but parliamentary institutions had little power in Imperial Germany and the government was dominated by conservative forces.

One sector of the economy was left largely untouched by this rapid industrialisation: agriculture. Germany remained a leading agrarian power. In contrast to Britain, where the proportion of the labour force working on the land was already very low by the turn of the century, in Germany over 35% of workers were still on the land on the eve of the First World War, and by 1939 the figure was still as high as 25%. Many of Germany's problems stemmed from the conflicts between industry and a persistently depressed agricultural sector.

In addition to imperial Germany's social and economic tensions there was a sense of frustrated nationalism. The creation of the empire in 1871 did not satisfy all German national aspirations because it did not include all Germans. More particularly Germany, even as a great continental state, did not seem to compare favourably with other European empires of the period. In the years up to 1914 Germany's bid for world power, by building a navy to challenge that of Britain and seeking colonies in Africa and elsewhere, largely proved a failure. Britain was able to outbuild the Germans and retained naval supremacy. The German national destiny therefore remained frustrated.

Finally, imperial Germany continued to be dominated by a narrow élite. The Prussian Junkers remained a dominant political force. Linked with them were the industrial élites of western Germany, who were equally antipathetic to radical political change. Germany therefore presented a paradox, a modernising country still run on very conservative lines. These social élites did not disappear with defeat in the First World War.

The 'stab in the back'

The importance of the second main element in the crisis that faced Weimar, the impact of the First World War, must also be emphasised. Germany's defeat in the war was unexpected, at least by the mass of the population though not, by the end of the war, by the German military. In November 1918 German troops were still on French and Belgian soil, in much the same place as they had been for the past four years. They had also won a massive victory in the east, totally defeating the Russian empire and dictating humiliating peace terms to the Bolshevik regime in early 1918 at Brest-Litovsk. Large parts of eastern Europe remained under German control at the end of the war. How then were the population to explain their defeat? The answer that proved plausible to many of them was that Germany had been stabbed in the back. This was a legend deliberately fostered by the conservative élites and particularly by the military. They portrayed Germany as having been defeated not by the allied armies but by internal enemies: the socialists, the Jews and any other convenient scapegoats.

The First World War was not just lost in the sense of a military defeat. It was also a war in which Germany had suffered very greatly, not least in comparison with other European countries. There was genuine hunger as a result of the Allied blockade which, incidentally, was maintained until Germany signed the Treaty of Versailles in mid-1919. But all the German sacrifices seemed in the end to have been for nothing.

Weaknesses at birth

The end of the war coincided with revolution at home. The revolution did not overthrow the regime: it had already been overthrown by military defeat, and had turned itself into a constitutional monarchy by late October 1918. The revolution started in an almost accidental fashion with a sailors' mutiny and then spread to other parts of Germany. It led to the abdication of the Kaiser and the proclamation of a German republic, but it was far from a full social revolution. The Social Democrats came to power in 1918 but they too were not, except for a small minority, in any sense revolutionary. One of the central questions which has been asked by historians of the Weimar Republic is whether those who came to power at that time could have done more to strengthen its political and social bases, and done more to deal with the entrenched powers of the army, the aristocracy and the bureaucracy. Most of them, however, had no revolutionary intent. Indeed the first Chancellor, and later first President of the new republic, the Social Democratic leader Friedrich Ebert, declared that he 'hated the revolution like sin'. He and his colleagues did not want to see 'Russian conditions' in Germany. They therefore opposed the extreme left, as represented by factions that had split away from the

SPD, such as the Spartakist League led by Rosa Luxemburg and Karl Liebknecht. The SPD were more frightened of the far left than they were of the military and the right, and did a deal with the army in order to defeat the extreme left. The Spartakist uprising of January 1919 was put down with extreme brutality.

The constitution produced by Germany's new rulers was highly democratic. It was drawn up at the small town of Weimar, a fairly safe place to be in troubled times when Berlin was extremely unsafe. The Weimar constitution entailed almost perfect democracy and had the defects of its perfection. Proportional representation allowed minority parties to have access to the Reichstag, and it was easy for the chamber to overturn governments by votes of no confidence. At the same time Article 48 of the constitution put tremendous powers in the hands of the President in times of emergency. In practice emergencies ran for years at a time. Article 48 was used many times by President Ebert between 1919 and 1923. It was used again continuously after 1929. The democratic constitution of Weimar therefore also had this built-in authoritarian element.

Defeat and internal crises

Weimar was, however, being shaped in the period of crisis, both economic and political, that hit Germany immediately after the First World War. The war was of course an expensive business and, like everybody else, the Germans had hoped to pay for it by extracting money from those they had beaten. In the event it was the Germans who had to pay the enormous sums of reparations fixed by the western allies. This placed a great burden on the German economy.

In addition there was the problem of inflation. Inflation was already endemic during the war and became more serious still afterwards, and especially in 1923. In that year the French and Belgians occupied the Ruhr, the main industrial area of Germany, and the German government simply printed money in order to support the passive resistance to the French. Hyper-inflation that resulted meant that banknotes became increasingly worthless, with vast amounts necessary to buy simple necessities. The hyper-inflation hit most severely not the working class, but the fixed incomes and the savings of the middle class. This was a very powerful element in alienating an important social group from the regime.

In 1919–23 there were also the political crises presented by attacks on the republic from both left and right. Following the suppression of the Spartakist revolt in January 1919, a succession of further communist risings were put down very efficiently by the German army. In addition there were right-wing attempts to seize power. In 1920 a former bureaucrat, Dr Kapp, led a rising which so frightened the government that they left Berlin. It was only the refusal of the civil service to cooperate with the leaders of the putsch, and a general strike, which brought it to an end. The next major right-wing coup attempt was in Munich in November 1923, led by Hitler and by the war hero General Ludendorff. This ended in ignominious failure when the Munich police had the nerve to fire on the rebels. Hitler was put on trial and imprisoned for a few months, where he lived in comfortable conditions and had the leisure to write his political testament *Mein Kampf*.

The Hitler putsch marked the end of the period of direct challenges to the state from the extreme left and extreme right. However, important social groups remained unreconciled to the republic, the more so as their economic position continued to be undermined – particularly in the agricultural sector, which was in a state of almost permanent depression throughout the 1920s. This meant that even though the economy stabilised after 1923, promoting a period of relative political peace, any destabilisation would reawaken fears of a return to hyper-inflation and political crisis.

Stabilising the Republic

The crises of 1919–23 helped to maintain the resentment against the Versailles treaty which had been imposed on Germany by the Allies, both because of the problems that were felt to flow from it and because of the affront to German nationalism it represented, not least in its war guilt clauses. However in the mid-1920s there were more encouraging signs, both at home and abroad. The German economy stabilised very rapidly in 1923–24 with the aid of the introduction of a new currency unit, the Reichsmark. The restoration of business confidence was assisted by foreign financial aid, especially from the United States. Under the Dawes Plan of 1924, which brought about a partial solution to the reparations problem, large amounts of American money flowed into Germany. However, the recovery that followed disguised considerable structural weaknesses in the German economy, not least in the position of agriculture. It was also a fragile recovery in the sense that the funds which made it possible, the foreign loans, could be withdrawn very rapidly. This was indeed beginning to happen even before the Wall Street Crash of October 1929.

In 1923–29 the political scene also looked much more encouraging. At the beginning of the 1920s when the republic was founded, many important political groups were hostile to it, especially amongst those on the right. They included the German People's

Party and the more right-wing German National People's Party. Both of these parties, the former led by the dominant figure in the politics of the late 1920s, Gustav Stresemann, came round to supporting the republic. Admittedly the German nationalists did so mainly for tactical reasons. This development did mean, however, that there was now broad support for the republic, ranging from the Social Democrats to the Nationalists. The only parties which remained wholly unreconciled to the republic at this stage were the Communists and the Nazis, but, in electoral terms at least, neither party carried much weight in this period. One notable symbol of republican consolidation was the election of the war hero, Paul von Hindenburg, as President in 1925. His election helped to reconcile the right to the republic, but also indicated how far the republic had moved away from the democratic and socialist aspirations of its founders.

International developments in this period were also favourable. Germany had been treated as an outcast at Versailles. By the mid-1920s Germany was no longer despised and isolated. The key figure here was Stresemann, the German foreign minister from 1923 until his death in 1929. He negotiated the Locarno treaties of 1925 which brought Germany into the European security system. In particular he promoted reconciliation with France. The result was considerable progress towards the dismantling of the Versailles settlement. In 1929 the Young Plan brought a mutually satisfactory solution of the reparations question. The following year the last Allied troops left the Rhineland.

The economic blizzard

By then the overall picture was encouraging. There was considerable prosperity under a Social Democrat-led government and the recovery of Germany's international position, symbolised not least by admittance to the League of Nations in 1926. But this encouraging scenario was to collapse very quickly. In October 1929 the American stock market boom collapsed. Stresemann died in the same month. Both of these events were of great significance, the one in destabilising the German economy and the other by removing a stabilising political influence.

In March 1930 the last democratic government of the Weimar Republic was replaced by one which did not have a parliamentary majority, led by Heinrich Brüning. Later in 1930 the Nazis achieved their first significant electoral success. In 1931 the economy was further hit by a major financial crisis. The following year Brüning's government fell. It was replaced by that of von Papen, and then, after only a few months, by von Schleicher. His short-lived administration ended when the Nazis were manoeuvred into power on 30 January 1933.

The fall of the republic might not have come about if the depression had not been so severe and so prolonged. Given a longer period of economic success Weimar might have gained general acceptance among the German people, just as the German Federal Republic was to do after 1949.

Brüning and the beginning of the end

Once the slump had begun, however, the Weimar Republic's chances of survival were much diminished. Whether its fate was inevitable, and in particular whether there were any viable alternatives to the policies pursued by Brüning after 1930, have been the subject of intense debate among historians. On the one hand Brüning has been seen as a sincere statesman trying to stabilise German democracy, though admittedly at fault for an overly deflationary economic policy. As early as 1935, however, the left-wing historian Arthur Rosenburg described the formation of Brüning's government as the beginning of the end of German democracy. His reputation further suffered, ironically, through the posthumous publication of his memoirs in 1970, from which it became clear that his preference was for a more authoritarian form of government, possibly a restoration of the monarchy. More disturbing is the evidence from his memoirs that Brüning was deliberately intensifying the economic crisis for particular political ends. Cardinal amongst these was the aim of persuading the Allies that Germany could no longer pay reparations. This was an extremely risky strategy, but one which was to a certain extent successful. The British, at least, were convinced, as the diaries of the then British Prime Minister, Ramsay MacDonald, show. The Hoover moratorium on reparations was introduced in 1931, and reparations were finally swept away at the Lausanne conference in August 1932, shortly after Brüning's dismissal.

Clearly however, Brüning can be accused of having made a disastrous mistake in calling a general election in September 1930. There was no need for an election then, as the previous one had only been in 1928, but of course he was trying to achieve a majority in the Reichstag. What it brought instead was a Nazi electoral breakthrough. The Nazis advanced from the 12 seats they had won in 1928 to 107. They were now the second largest party in the Reichstag and clearly had to be included in all future political calculations. Lying behind this electoral success was not so much the economic situation, which had not then reached peak intensity, as the success of Nazi party-building at the grass roots since 1925.

After its refoundation in 1925 the party became a national party for the first time, rather than one merely of southern Germany. It gained a growing membership, dedicated to spreading the Nazi word throughout Germany. It is this growing support that helps to explain the party's electoral success in 1930.

Brüning, like his successors up to 1933, was trying above all to achieve legitimacy and to secure a majority in the Reichstag. The debates and intrigues as to how to construct this majority were a key element in the politics of the period 1930–33. They indicated that the conservative governments of the period were at least paying lip-service to the requirements of the democratic constitution. More than this, they were acknowledging that they needed a popular mandate to pursue their solutions for Germany's economic and political problems. None of them was prepared to ride roughshod over German democracy, as Hitler was to do, but all were seeking to replace it with a more authoritarian solution – one more suited to troubled times and also more in tune with German traditions, as they saw them.

The establishment of a 'liberal dictatorship' might have been a sensible solution but no politician – except, possibly, von Schleicher – wanted that, least of all Hitler. Hitler was the politician who, having been involved in the failed putsch of 1923, saw most clearly that power could not be seized by a coup, and that the ballot box had to be used to overthrow democracy. Superficially, therefore, his object was the same as that of constitutional politicians: to build up electoral support and win a majority in the Reichstag. Unless they were able or willing to enter into partnership with other parties, the Nazis thus had to win more than 50% of the vote.

Undermining democracy

All politicians were thus trying to secure a majority. That this was not an easy task was not merely the politicians' fault; it was also that of the voters. The electorate was turning away from the democratic parties, and even from the parties of the 'constitutional right'. After 1930 there was growing support for the Communists and a much larger growth in support for the Nazis. The July 1932 election saw a massive increase in both Communist and Nazi votes. The significance of this election should not be overlooked. It can be seen as marking a massive swing towards the Nazis and the high point of their success under free electoral conditions. This was not, however, how it was seen at the time. Instead the focus was on the slowing down of the rate of increase in the Nazi level of support and the much more rapid rise in the vote for the Communists, who appeared much more threatening than the Nazis in the eyes of 'respectable' opinion. In July 1932 the Communists won 14.5% of the vote and the Nazis 37.4%. This meant that a majority of the votes (51.9%) and of the seats in the Reichstag had been won by anti-democratic parties.

Accordingly it was impossible for the constitutional parties, from Junkers to Social Democrats, to construct a parliamentary majority. However, their electoral success still did not mean that the Nazis could form a government. It was a phenomenally successful election for them, as they won the hightest share of the popular vote won by any party under the Weimar constitution. It did not, however, give Hitler a majority or an automatic right to claim the Chancellorship, as he found to his cost when he tried to claim the post in August 1932, only to be refused by President Hindenburg. The problem for Hitler as 1932 wore on was that he was losing support and was in danger of political extinction. Von Papen was gambling on this when he called yet another general election for November 1932. The Nazi share of the vote fell significantly to 33.1% and the party was in a state of internal crisis. Hitler's strategy appeared to have failed.

The final political crisis

In late 1932 conservative politicians on the one hand were trying to construct a parliamentary majority, while on the other Hitler was becoming increasingly desperate to attain power. The responsibility for the demise of the Weimar Republic and the triumph of Nazism must lie not only with the electorate but also with those figures who played into Hitler's hands and manoeuvred him into the Chancellorship. Here our focus shifts to a very small group of people, hardly any of whom held elected office. This concentration of power in a small coterie in itself indicates the decay of the Weimar Republic. This group of key figures includes the 84-year-old President Hindenburg, the former Chancellor (August–November 1932) Franz von Papen, the President's son, Oskar von Hindenburg, as well as members of the German military high command (General von Blomberg for instance) and assorted industrialists and landowners.

Another figure to be mentioned is the then (and last) Chancellor of the Republic, General Kurt von Schleicher. Schleicher is one of the most intriguing figures in Weimar history. He was an unscrupulous but in some respects engaging character, perhaps too intelligent for his own good. On the one hand Schleicher bears a primary responsibility for the downfall of German democracy. It was he who brought Brüning to power in 1930 – a deliberate undermining of democracy to put in power a government which was accountable only to the President and which ruled by Presidential decree. More than that, Schleicher was a crucial advocate of the idea of taming the Nazis by bringing them into government. From the Nazi electoral success in 1930 onwards, Schleicher was trying to bring Nazis into government in some way, in the belief that their extremism would be modified once they had tasted power.

In support of this view he drew on two important historical lessons; both of them, as it turned out, misread. One was the treatment of the Socialists under Bismarck. Bismarck had persecuted the Socialists and this had made them stronger. Schleicher therefore drew the moral that it was better to accommodate than to persecute the Nazis. The second lesson he drew on was that of the British Labour government of 1924. He saw this as a case of a radical party being tamed by responsibility. Labour however, unlike the Nazis, was never an anti-constitutional party. Seeing parallels between the two parties was a catastrophic misjudgement. Eventually, very belatedly, Schleicher realised this.

It is here that we see the positive side of Schleicher's political career. When he became Chancellor in early December 1932 he was fully aware of the Nazi danger and was trying to avert it. He attempted a new approach, 'the policy of the diagonal', drawing a line from the left to the right. Schleicher aimed to link up with the trade unions on the one hand, and on the other with the 'moderate' Nazis grouped around Gregor Strasser. The unions did not trust him and he could not undermine Strasser's loyalty to Hitler. At the same time he was losing the support of industrialists, who thought him too radical, and of the army, who feared civil war and did not want to be placed in a position where they had to fire on Nazis. Finally Schleicher lost the support of the President, who rightly blamed him for undermining the previous Chancellor, von Papen.

The end of Weimar

When Schleicher failed in his radical strategy the opportunity was open to those who saw Nazism as a means of legitimating a conservative alternative to the Weimar Republic, and who felt, in the light of its internal divisions and weakening electoral perform- ance, that they would be able to contain it. Papen and his associates aimed at a conservative, nationalist, anti-democratic state, perhaps resembling the regime established around the same time by Salazar in Portugal and later by Franco in Spain, and they thought they would be able to control and manipulate Hitler. In order to get Hitler into government they offered him the Chancellorship, the office from which he had always previously been excluded. They then had to persuade the President. Ironically Hindenburg was the last guardian of Weimar democracy.

The conservatives, having won round Hindenburg, thought that they could control the new government. There were only three Nazis in the cabinet: Hitler as Chancellor, Frick as Minister of the Interior and Goering as Minister without Portfolio. Those responsible for this accession to power could not have envisaged the eventual fruits of their manoeuvres, the years of war and the gas chambers. However Hitler's anti-democratic intentions had already been made clear, not merely in *Mein Kampf*, which few of these aristocratic intriguers had consulted, but also in his speeches, and in the speeches of other Nazi party leaders. The brutality of the Nazis was also already evident from the street violence which they had fostered. There was no ambiguity about the Nazis' intention of using democracy in order to destroy it. It seems equally clear that a large section of the German population who voted for them, as well as important elements in the German establishment, had the same intention.

How is this readiness to ditch democracy to be explained? Germany had undergone defeat, followed by traumatic economic crises, both of which had undermined the legitimacy of the Weimar Republic. But the rejection of democracy also reflects defects of the German political culture of the time. Arnold Brecht, a German bureaucrat of the old school (who also happened to be a convinced Social Democrat), wrote in his memoirs (*The Political Education of Arnold Brecht*) of 'the political immaturity, ignorance and short-sightedness of the average German citizen regarding the special risk of uncontrolled authoritarian government'. Spared the arbitrary government and civil war of seventeenth-century England or the absolutism of the French *ancien régime*, the Germans 'were entirely blind to the dangers threatening their nation and themselves if they were to transfer unlimited power to one man or group.' If Weimar had some chances of survival before 1929, it had very little chance afterwards, not just because of the Slump but also because of the attitudes and actions of the German electorate and their political leaders.

This does not mean that Nazism was its inevitable replacement. Nazism came to power as a result of a miscalculation by conservative politicians and the military after a large number, but by no means a majority of the electorate, had put it in a position to contend for power. Those who intrigued Hitler into power were opposed to Weimar democracy and favoured a return to authoritarianism, but they neither wanted nor expected the triumph of Nazism.

Patrick Salmon lectures in History at the University of Newcastle-upon-Tyne.

Alan Bullock
Personality in History: Hitler and Stalin

A perennial A-level dilemma is how to explain the rise of Hitler and Stalin and the horrors that were carried out under their rules. Drawing on his recent research, Alan Bullock offers some clues.

I do not believe that either Hitler or Stalin created the historical circumstances of which they were able to take advantage. Nor was there anything inevitable about the rise of either man. Neither would have succeeded had it not been for a stroke of luck. In Stalin's case this was the unexpected death of Lenin at the early age of 54; in Hitler's the unexpected chance offered by the economic depression which hit Germany with such force that it allowed him to convert the Nazi vote of 800,000 in the election of 1928 to over 6 million in 1930, and to double that again to over 13 million in 1932.

Men of destiny

The motivation of both men was a passion to dominate, a need to dominate, which they combined with a belief about themselves that they were men of destiny, destined to play a great role in the world. In both cases this belief was linked to a feeling about history. Stalin derived his sense of mission from an identification with the creed of Marxism-Leninism, a creed he believed had uncovered the laws of historical development of which he was to be the agent.

Hitler too saw his destiny as a part of history. 'I often wonder,' he said, 'why the ancient world collapsed.' He thought the explanation was Christianity, the invention of the Jew, Saul of Tarsus, better known as St Paul, who had played the same disintegrative role in the ancient world as Bolshevism, the invention of the Jew, Karl Marx, had in the modern. He saw himself having been born in a time of crisis similar to that of the ancient world, at a time when the liberal bourgeois order of the nineteenth century was disintegrating and when the future would lie with the egalitarian Jewish-Bolshevik ideology of the Marxist-led masses, unless Europe could be saved by the Nazi racist ideology of the new elite which it was his mission to create.

Hitler was quite open in what he had to say about himself. He spoke of himself confidently as a man called by Providence to raise

Germany from the humiliation of defeat in 1918 – the first stage of re-creating a new racist empire in the east of Europe. His great gift was as a speaker, arguably the greatest demagogue in history. No one has described the charismatic attraction someone like Hitler could exercise on an audience better than Nietzsche, 11 years before Hitler was born:

> Men believe in the truth of all that is seen to be strongly believed. In all great deceivers a remarkable process is at work to which they owe their power. In the very act of deception with all its preparations, the dreadful voice, the expressions, the gestures, they are overcome by their belief in themselves and it is this belief which then speaks so persuasively, so miracle-like to the audience.

And Nietzsche added: 'not only does he communicate that to the audience but the audience returns it to him and strengthens his belief.'

Stalin's seizure of power

Stalin presents an entirely different picture. At some stage, he formed the same conviction as Hitler that he was destined to play a great role in history. Unlike Hitler, however, Stalin had to keep this belief to himself. The Bolshevik Party, as good Marxists, were deeply hostile to anything like a cult of personality. For Stalin to allow any hint to appear of his conviction that he had a historic role to play would have been fatal to his advancement.

While Hitler had to create his own party and win mass support in a series of open elections, Stalin had been carried into office by the October Revolution of 1917, in which he played a minor role, and owed his subsequent promotion as General Secretary of the party to Lenin's favour. His chance came by an extraordinary piece of luck when Lenin died in January 1924, at the early age of 54, just when he realised that he had made a mistake and was planning to revoke Stalin's appointment. The least fancied of the contestants for the succession, Stalin possessed none of Hitler's charismatic gifts. They would have been counterproductive with the audience he had to win, the closed world of the central bodies of the Soviet Communist Party. Declaring that no one could take Lenin's place, he called for a collective leadership, in which he succeeded in establishing his own claim to be, not Lenin's successor, but the guardian of his legacy.

In Stalin's hands this was enough to enable him to out-manoeuvre his rivals (above all Trotsky) by accusing them of abandoning

Leninist principles and branding them as guilty of factionalism and of dividing the party in pursuit of personal ambition. At the same time he used his position as General Secretary of the party to manipulate appointments to the *nomenklatura*, the 5,500 leading party office holders – such as regional secretaries – who effectively governed the huge country. By this means, during the 1920s, Stalin built up a body of clients (to borrow a term from Roman history) who knew very well on whom they depended for preferment and what was expected of them in return.

By the end of 1939 each man had achieved a unique position which admitted no rivals and no opposition. The revolution which Stalin had imposed on the Russian peoples between his fiftieth and his sixtieth year (1929–39) had completed the work left incomplete when Lenin died. Stalin was already coming to see his revolution as a continuation of the historic tradition of the tsarist state. But in laying claim to be the successor to Peter the Great, he refused to abandon the claim to the revolutionary succession as well. It was the combination of these two traditions, the Marxist-Leninist-ideological, with the Russian-nationalist, both refracted through the medium of Stalin's own personality, which characterised the Stalinist state. In 1939 Hitler, 10 years younger, had still to complete his revolution, but he had taken a decisive step towards it by freeing himself of dependence on the traditional German elites who had helped him into power; by restoring Germany's dominant position in Central Europe with the occupation of Austria and Czechoslovakia, and by breaking through the barrier between peace and war with the attack on Poland.

Great men in history

But how far, you may ask, were these personal achievements? Are they not rather to be seen as the product of socio-historical forces which both in Russia and in Germany would have produced the same result, whoever was nominally in command? Certainly neither series of changes would have been possible without the commitment and active participation of a great number of other men; no individual, however gifted, could have carried them out by himself. In the process had Stalin and Hitler not become prisoners of the systems and bureaucracies it had been necessary to create; were they any more than figureheads, whose continuation in office depended upon their continuing to satisfy the expectations of their supporters? How could it be otherwise? In the modern world, with its huge populations and complex organisation, surely no individual can exert an influence upon the course of history comparable with that exercised by rulers in earlier times – for example the Tsar Peter the Great and the Prussian King Frederick the Great, with whom Stalin and Hitler identified – when the scale of events and the forces engaged were so much smaller.

As a general proposition, in the settled societies in which we live, yes: who could disagree with it? But let us look a little more closely at the nature of the power Stalin and Hitler exercised. There was, of course, a great difference in style between them. Stalin was the more reserved, Hitler the more flamboyant; Stalin operated in the shadows, Hitler performed best in the limelight. Stalin was more the calculator, Hitler the gambler. The Georgian was *un homme de gouvernement*, the experienced administrator, disciplining himself to regular work; the Austrian still the artist-politician, hating routine. The style was different but the nature of the power they exercised was the same, personal power inherent in the man not the office. The only office Stalin held until 1941 was as General Secretary of the Soviet Communist Party. It was the fact that Stalin held it, that made this the most important office in the Soviet Union. Only with the war did he become formally head of government and Supreme Commander.

Stalin's power was not only personal, but also concealed. The 'cult of personality' increasingly projected him as of more than human stature; but it was part of the fiction necessary, if he was to continue to lay claim to the Marxist-Leninist as well as the tsarist succession, that this should be presented as the spontaneous tribute of the Russian people, embarrassing to a man, sprung from the Russian people, who asked no more than to serve them and the party as its general secretary. The formula employed for any decision was impersonal, 'the "highest Soviet authorities" have decided'; the secret was all the more powerful because everyone in office knew that this meant Stalin, but that this must never be mentioned in public.

At first sight, Hitler's position was exactly the opposite: head of state, head of government, head of party and supreme commander, all combined in the unique title of Führer of the German People. But it was the fact that Adolf Hitler was the Führer that gave the office its authority, just as it was the fact Stalin held it that made the office of General Secretary of the party the most important in the Soviet Union. The only difference was that this was concealed in Stalin's case, but openly acknowledged in Hitler's.

The exercise of power

The fact that Hitler's and Stalin's power was personal in character was no guarantee, however, that it was effective, was real not formal power. We have still to go on and ask, what was the relationship between the two individual leaders and the massive bureaucracies which were characteristic of both Communist Russia and Nazi Germany. Having created a unique position of authority for himself, Hitler was determined not to see it institutionalised or defined. The Weimar constitution was never formally replaced: the constitutional rights of the citizen were only 'suspended' by emergency decree, never repealed. The sole basis of the Nazi regime was a single law, the Enabling Act, passed by the Reichstag in March 1933, giving the cabinet the power to enact laws. As the cabinet met less and less frequently and not at all after February 1938, this meant Hitler; in fact, laws were soon replaced by decrees.

But Hitler was not interested in the day-to-day business of government, and more and more withdrew from it, concentrating his attention on his long-term interests of foreign policy, rearmament and war. To a degee unthinkable in the case of Stalin, he left the more powerful of the Nazi leaders – Goering, Himmler, Goebbels, Ley – free not only to build up rival empires but to feud with each other and with the established ministries in a continuing fight to take over parts of each other's territory. The result has been variously described as 'authoritarian anarchy', 'permanent improvisation', 'administrative chaos' – very different from the outside world's picture of a monolithic totalitarian state.

Such a state of affairs suited Hitler very well, allowing him to make arbitrary interventions, whenever he chose to, so keeping the civil service uncertain of his intentions. At the same time he outflanked it by setting up special agencies for tasks he regarded as urgent. The two most powerful of these were the Four Year Plan headed by Goering – which absorbed an increasing share of the German economy and eventually the economies of the occupied countries as well, with the priority for rearmament that Hitler demanded – and the fusion of the police and the *Gestapo* (secret police) with Himmler's SS empire. This removed the police function and the power of coercion from the state, placing it in the hands of a body unknown to the constitution and responsible only to Hitler himself.

Unlike Hitler, who detested administration and absented himself from his Chancellery for long periods, Stalin rarely left the Kremlin and demanded that his secretariat keep him informed of everything. But like Hitler he was determined not to let his power be defined or regularised. For him, too, power, to be effective, had to be arbitrary and intervention unpredictable – at any level he chose, from top to bottom of the bureaucratic hierarchy.

This is the key to the extraordinary series of purges and show trials launched by Stalin in 1936–39. On the pretext of defending the Bolshevik Party and the Leninist tradition, Stalin wiped out the generation of leaders – his own generation – who had known and served with Lenin. Accusing them of betraying the cause to which they had devoted their lives, he replaced them with a rising younger generation – Khrushchev's and Brezhnev's generation – who had never known Lenin or any other leader than Stalin. Stalin extended the purges to the Red Army and navy, the state ministries, the nationalised industries, and the cultural establishment as well as the party hierarchy. The security police, the NKVD, provided Stalin, as the Gestapo-SS provided Hitler, with an instrument specially created to carry out arbitrary decisions, responsible solely to him personally, operating outside the law and licensed to use any degree of force necessary, including torture and death. And with a twist characteristic of Stalin, the NKVD itself was subject to the purge: those who carried out the interrogations and secured confessions by torture knew all the time that they might be cast in the role of victim, not executioner. All told, the number of those arrested in 1937 and 1938 was of the order of 7–8 million, of whom around one million died in the camps. The intensity of the purges in the late 1930s could not be maintained without dangerously weakening the Soviet Union. But the purge was not abandoned; instead of an emergency measure, Stalin made it into a permanent feature of Soviet life.

The maintenance of personal power

Let me try to draw together the threads of my argument. I have sought to show that, once they came to power, neither Stalin nor Hitler had any intention of letting themselves become prisoners of a system. What they made sure of was that their power remained inherent in the man, not the office. This does not mean that they decided everything – that was impossible – but that they were free to decide anything which they chose, and that they could do this, without warning, without consulting or requiring the agreement of anyone else. Of course Stalin and Hitler do not bear the sole responsibility for the actions, crimes and mistakes committed during these years. Millions of men and women were involved, in the Soviet Union, in Germany and as collaborators in the occupied countries. From the operations on the ground, responsibility reached up through the bureaucratic hierarchies where the thousands of 'little Hitlers' and 'little Stalins' abused their power without waiting for orders from above, to Hitler's and Stalin's closest associates, Molotov, Kaganovich, Beria; Goering, Himmler and Bormann. Neither Hitler nor Stalin, so far as is known, ever witnessed or personally took part in the acts of terror and repression which were not peripheral but absolutely central to the exercise and preservation of their power. Nonetheless, their responsibility was of a different kind from and greater than that of anyone else. I shall illustrate my argument with half a dozen examples.

The first is the collectivisation of Russian agriculture. Russia was overwhelmingly a peasant country: 80% of its population, 120 million people, lived in 600,000 villages. At some stage, if the Communist programme was to be carried out, the land had to be taken out of peasant ownership and nationalised. Stalin won support in the party because he argued that this could not be put off, but no one ever supposed that he would attempt to carry it out and collectivise the 25 million peasant holdings in one or at most two years – a social upheaval on a scale for which there is no parallel in history except Mao's Great Leap Forward, which was modelled on it. It could only be accomplished by force, Stalin's revolution from above. The human cost is estimated at 11 million lives, with another 3.5 million dying in the labour camps later; 5 million of that total was due to a man-made famine which Stalin deliberately imposed on the Ukraine in order to break peasant resistance. The whole Communist Party as well as the security forces and the army were involved, but the driving force behind collectivisation, the will to complete it in four years, whatever the cost, was Stalin's – and Russian agriculture has never recovered from the methods he used.

My second example follows on from the first. Although muted, there was criticism of Stalin's methods in the party, and a move at the 1934 Party Congress – the details of which remain obscure – to replace him with Kirov. The move failed and an open split was avoided. But Stalin did not forget. In December 1934 Kirov was assassinated (almost certainly on Stalin's initiative) and over the next two years Stalin made his preparations for the series of purges and trials which I have already described. Stalin, like Hitler in the Holocaust, took care to conceal his role, but even the evidence we already have leaves no doubt that *Pravda* was right when it declared in April 1988: 'Stalin did not simply know, he organised and directed the purges. Today this is a fact, already proved.' Amongst the proofs are 383 lists of names – in all, 40,000 names – which required and received Stalin's personal signature for execution.

Hitler and war

The fact that Hitler suppressed the radical wing of the Nazi Party in 1934 when it called for a 'second revolution' misled many at the time – and some historians since – into believing that he was not to be taken seriously as a revolutionary. Hitler meant to have his revolution all right, but instead of turning aggression inwards and setting one class against another, he meant to turn the energies and tensions of the German people outwards and create a racist empire at the expense of the Slav *Untermenschen* ('sub-humans') in the East, so providing the Germans, far better than any internal revolution could, with the psychological satisfaction as well as the material advantages of a *Herrenvolk* ('master-race'). This programme was plainly set out in *Mein Kampf*, published in the mid-1920s.

Until he could carry out the re-armament to which he gave overriding priority, however, Hitler had to lull suspicions abroad and keep the support of the conservative-nationalist forces in Germany. There was no timetable or blueprint of aggression; Hitler was both a gambler and an opportunist, but never lost sight of his ultimate objective. By the winter of 1937–38 he had made sufficient progress to change the terms of the game and raise the stakes. Dismissing the banker Schacht as Minister of Economics and the conservative leaders of the foreign ministry and the army, he went over to the offensive with the annexation of Austria and the destruction of the Czechoslovak state. The first was an improvisation, the second so alarmed the German army that a plot was mounted to arrest Hitler and only called off when Chamberlain offered to fly to Munich. Six months later Hitler entered Prague without a gun being fired.

Hitler's object, however, was not to avoid war; he believed war was essential if he was to re-arm the German people psychologically (*Wiederwehrheftmachung*, his own phrase) for the conquest of empire. The key was to isolate those Powers which opposed him and defeat them one at a time in a series of single campaigns. The diplomatic coup of the Nazi-Soviet Pact, relieving him of any threat of Soviet intervention in case of war, was not only the outstanding example of such a strategy but provides the clearest possible illustration of both men's personal authority. For only leaders completely confident of their hold on power and free to act without consultation could have taken the risk of openly reversing the policies with which they were identified at home and abroad – Hitler's defence of European civilisation against Communism, Stalin's leadership of the anti-fascist crusade.

The gain for Stalin was the partition of Poland and the annexation of territory in Eastern Europe larger than France; for Hitler it was a free hand in defeating first the Poles, then the French. With the destruction of Poland, Hitler had carried the German people, still mindful of defeat in 1918, over the psychological barrier between peace and war. It was followed by the defeat of France and the eviction of Britain from the continent, raising him to a peak of personal success which no German leader before him had equalled. In achieving this, Hitler acted in defiance of the General Staff's advice, scrapping their plan for the French campaign in favour of one which they had rejected. The effect was to convince Hitler of the infallibility of his judgement in war as in politics. On 31 July 1940 he ordered the army to prepare plans for an attack on Russia the following May (1941) which would destroy the Soviet state in a campaign of five months. Hitler never wanted a war with the British, whom he admired for their success in creating an empire; all he asked was that they should give up any pretension to interfere in Europe. When the British refused, and the defeat of the German air force in the Battle of Britain convinced him that invasion would be a risky gamble, he decided to ignore them and go ahead with his real objective from the beginning, the attack on Russia.

While Hitler became more and more irked by the Nazi-Soviet Pact, Stalin did all in his power to prolong it by increasing Soviet supplies to Germany of raw materials and food to levels which Russia could ill afford to spare. In the face of a flood of evidence that the Germans were concentrating their forces for an invasion of Russia, Stalin persisted in believing that Hitler would not attack before 1942–43, and that the Western powers were trying to trick him into provoking Hitler by counter-measures. The Russian commanders were not allowed to order defensive preparations right up to and including the night of 21/22 June.

That night, the largest army ever assembled for a single campaign, 3,200,000 troops broke across the frontiers, driving to the outskirts of Leningrad and Moscow, overrunning the Ukraine and, in the second half of 1941, capturing three million prisoners, most of whom were so badly treated by the Germans that they died. This was the price of Stalin's obstinacy, compounding the unprecedented blows he had dealt to the Soviet military leadership during the purges. Not until German troops had reached the oilfields of the Caucasus, and the Red Army was fighting desperately to hold Stalingrad on the Volga in the winter of 1942–43, would Stalin's distrust of the officer corps allow an alternative military leadership to emerge.

War in the East

Hitler left it to the German army to carry out the preparations for the attack on Russia. But the decision to make such an attack was Hitler's alone, taken without consultation or discussion. Hitler's gamble was that the Soviet state was so much weakened by the purges that it would collapse – as the French had done – if subjected to a series of violent blows compressed into a single campaigning season. It is possible that the gamble might have come off, had he not rejected the army plan to continue the advance on Moscow after the capture of Smolensk in mid-July, insisting that they should first complete the overrunning of the Ukraine. As a result the drive on Moscow was not resumed until 2 October at the beginning of autumn, instead of in the summer weather of August or even September. Certainly, it was in the middle of October that the Soviet resistance came nearest to cracking. But, once Hitler's original gamble failed to come off – and with the winter weather and the Russian counter-offensive of 5 December, this became certain – the odds against a German success grew longer and longer.

By an extraordinary effort of will-power, Hitler mastered the crisis, halted any German retreat and stabilised the front, still deep in Russian territory. But the lesson he drew from it, that so long as his will remained unbroken, he would still prevail, proved his undoing. His refusal to listen to advice, his conviction of his mission, his belief that Providence would never allow him to be defeated, which had combined to produce one success after another, now combined to produce one defeat after another. Doubling the stakes by gratuitously declaring war on the United States and renewing the offensive on the Eastern Front instead of going over to the defensive, he compounded his difficulties by brutal occupation policies, refusing to play the role of liberator from Stalin's oppression – for example, in the Ukraine – or alternatively, refusing to seek a compromise peace with Stalin which could have left him master of Europe, including the Ukraine, Byelorussia and the Baltic States. Instead he forced the German army, for nearly two and a half years after the defeat at Stalingrad, to fight step by step all the way back from the Volga to Berlin, a distance of 1,000 miles, with total disregard of the cost in human lives and of the consequences for Germany and Europe. The end result of Hitler's defence of European civilisation against Communism was to leave half of Europe and half of Germany under Soviet occupation and Communist rule for more than 40 years.

Hitler and the Holocaust

The attack on Russia enabled Hitler to bring together into a common focus his strategic, political and ideological objectives – the conquest of *Lebensraum* in the East, the defeat of egalitarian Marxism, the enslavement of the Slav *Untermenschen* and the 'Final Solution of the Jewish Problem'. Moscow was the capital and symbol of the Slav, Marxist and Jewish threat to the Ayran race. Persecution of the Jews had begun on the night Hitler became Chancellor; until the war, however, its object had been to strip German Jews of their possessions, deprive them of all rights and force them to emigrate. The turning point was the decision to invade Russia. Hitler insisted to the German commanders as well as to the SS that this was no ordinary clash of arms, but a conflict of two ideologies, a war of extermination, *Vernichtungskrieg*. If this was to be applied to ordinary Russian soldiers and civilians – as it was – it meant that the last inhibitions had been abandoned in the treatment of Russian Jews. But 'the total solution of the Jewish question' was aimed at more than the Jewish population of Poland and Russia – at nothing less than the extermination of the whole Jewish population of Europe, estimated by the Nazis at around 11 million.

The fact that there is no order signed by Hitler is not surprising. Careful as always of his public image with the German people, he had deliberately distanced himself from the anti-Jewish riots of November 1938, and from the secret wartime programme for killing the physically and mentally handicapped which he had authorised but immediately ordered stopped when it brought strong protests from the churches. The plan for exterminating the Jews was to be carried out in Poland and Russia, not Germany, and every effort made to keep it secret. Only those who needed to know were told by word of mouth that the order came from the Führer himself.

Hitler left it to Himmler, Heydrich and the SS to build the death camps and organise the transport to them of Jews from all over Europe; but there was only one man among the Nazi leaders who had the imagination – however twisted – to come up with so grandiose and bizarre a plan, not Himmler or Goering but Hitler. And if there was one year in which Hitler was capable of making the giant leap from imagining such a 'solution' as fantasy to imagining it as fact, it was 1941. This was the year in which he showed the same unique gift for translating into literal fact another fantasy, that of *Lebensraum* and the empire in the east, to be achieved by the invasion of Russia. He left the organisation of that to the army's General Staff, just as he left the organisation of the final solution to the SS. But if there had not been a Hitler to conceive of such projects and to convince others that they could actually take place, I believe neither would have happened.

Hitler's second contribution to the Holocaust was to legitimise it. Those involved knew, as Himmler told the SS, that 'this is a page of glory in our history which can never be written', but they also knew, as Himmler went on to tell them, that they were carrying out the orders of the man who, as Führer, held a supreme position of authority in the German Reich. Hitler's final contribution was to insist that the operation to hunt down Jews all over Europe, from Holland and France to Greece was to continue into the final stages of the war when everyone knew it was lost. As the Russians overran the death camps, those who had not yet been 'processed' were force-marched to Germany by the SS and shot on arrival. The last such death march took place in May 1945, after Hitler's suicide.

Some weeks earlier, sitting amid the ruins of his hopes in the Berlin bunker, the man who had first appeared in history 25 years earlier ranting about the Jewish problem, found consolation in the thought that this problem at least had been solved and that the world would be grateful to him for it.

Dreadful legacy

Hitler died by his own hand, defeated but unrepentant, still convinced of his sense of mission, regretting only that he had not had the time to carry it out. Stalin emerged victorious, but saw no more reason than Hitler to change his mind. He still believed that the Russian people could only be ruled by force and fear – and that he was the only man who knew how to do this.

No other people had suffered anything like the Russian losses in the war – between 20 and 25 million military and civilian dead. Those who survived sought hope in the widespread belief that life after the war would now be different, that the repressive regime under which they had lived would now be relaxed, after all the efforts and sacrifices they had made.

Stalin soon disillusioned them. This was no time for relaxation, he declared – all the vigilance of the NKVD was still needed to protect the state (for which, read Stalin) against its enemies within and without. The officers and men who had fought their way halfway across Europe, and the prisoners of war who had survived their brutal treatment by the Germans, found themselves on their return received not with gratitude but with suspicion. Hundreds of thousands of them were sent to the camps. The same treatment was meted out to the millions who had lived under German occupation or been deported to the Reich as slave labour. At the time of Stalin's death, 12 million are estimated to have been held in the camps, and Stalin had already launched yet another purge with the discovery of the so-called 'Doctors' Plot'.

Defeat cost the Germans a terrible price, but at least spared them – and the world – the perpetuation of the Nazi regime. Victory cost the Soviet peoples an even greater price, but did not liberate them. Nor did Stalin's death. The system he had imposed on them, although modified over time, lasted for nearly another 40 years, leaving them economically so crippled and politically divided that they face an unpredictable future.

The dominant trend in the postwar study of history has been the rise of social and economic history, of history 'seen from below', challenging the traditional concentration on political history, history seen 'from above'. Social and economic historians, like social scientists, have found it natural to seek historical explanations in terms of such impersonal factors as demographic changes, movements of population, the impact on society of industrialisation and technological innovation, and to concern themselves with human beings collectively as members of groups in which individual characteristics are submerged in the average. Such an approach is well-suited to countries like the United States, Britain and France, whose political institutions, despite their shortcomings, are democratic, countries where despite the rapidity of change, there is sufficient stability and prosperity to preserve a framework of normality, and where pretensions to inspired leadership are unlikely to survive exposure by sceptical media and press.

Conclusions

But a different situation arises when war, defeat, civil war, revolution or some other violent upheaval disrupt normality and continuity, as happened in Russia in 1917, and in Germany in the Depression of the early 1930s, so soon after the defeat of 1918 and the inflation that followed. In such a situation, I believe, it is possible for an individual to exert a powerful, even a decisive, influence on the way events develop and the policies which are followed. This is what happened in Russia when Lenin returned to Russia in 1917, saw that there was a vacuum of power and turned the Bolshevik Party round and in defiance of the Marxist schema seized power not by a revolution – that had to come later – but by a *coup d'état*.

Such occasions are not common. There are many more situations where, for lack of leadership, a crisis is never resolved and the opportunity for a decisive turn goes begging. The moment more often than not fails to find the right person, as it did in Russia in 1905. Where a leader does emerge, however, as happened for example with Kemal Pasha in Turkey, with Gandhi in India, or with Mao in China, the person can establish a position which allows their personality, their individual gifts and their views to assume an importance out of all proportion to normal experience. And, once established, it is very difficult to dislodge a leader from such a position, as the example of Saddam Hussein shows. I believe Hitler and Stalin to have been two such cases.

I said earlier that neither man created the circumstances which gave them their opportunity. But I do not believe that circumstances by themselves in some mysterious way produce the man; I do not believe that, if not Hitler and Stalin, then someone else would have seized the opportunity and the result would have been much the same. There are many ways of writing history, especially of such large scale and abnormal episodes as the history of Nazi Germany or Stalinist Russia. I submit that one which focuses on the roles of Hitler and Stalin is legitimate and is one that forms a necessary part of any attempt to understand what happened and why.

Let me leave you with a final provocative question. In any mental hospital you may expect to find patients who suffer from the delusion that they are called upon to play a great historic role in some form or another – and are completely incapacitated by it. Why in Stalin's and Hitler's case did the same belief provide so exceptional a psychological drive as to carry them to such peaks of success that it would be hard to omit them from any list, however short, of individuals who have had the greatest impact on the history of the twentieth century? Read my book and work out the answer for yourselves.

This article was based on the Waterstone Lecture given by Lord Bullock on 28 October 1991. Lord Bullock's book, *Hitler and Stalin: Parallel Lives*, was published by Harper Collins in 1991. A revised edition in paperback was published in 1993.

PART IV
The Weaknesses of the Democracies and the Descent to War

Few subjects have aroused such moral indignation as the origins of the Second World War. Michael Foot entitled his book on appeasement *The Guilty Men*; the Vichy government of France put its pre-war political leaders on trial (though it was always rather unclear whether they were being tried for starting the war or losing it). Over thirty years ago A. J. P. Taylor sought to break away from this tone of moral indignation with the characteristically provocative claim that, in the area of foreign policy, Hitler should be treated as an ordinary German statesman pursuing the same national interests as his predecessors. Only more recently have historians come round to the view that the leaders of Britain and France (Chamberlain and Daladier) might also deserve to be treated as ordinary statesmen pursuing their national interests rather than as unique examples of cowardice and stupidity.

The policy of the Western allies makes more sense when it is considered in three lights. Firstly, none of the statesmen involved in appeasing Hitler was exclusively concerned with foreign policy. Chamberlain and Daladier (the prime ministers who signed the Munich agreement with Hitler) had both made their reputations in national rather than international politics. Indeed Chamberlain (former Lord Mayor of Birmingham) and Daladier ('the Bull of Vaucluse') were both noted for their local preoccupations. Some historians have been rather contemptuous of such concerns. They contrast the aldermanic worthies of 1938 unfavourably with the detached aristocrats who dominated diplomacy in the nineteenth century. This criticism is unfair: attempts had been made to transfer power from diplomats to elected governments and parliaments precisely because of the disaster that the former were seen to have brought about in 1914. Besides, the realities of the 1930s were different from those of the nineteenth century. Economic and social affairs could no longer be ignored and, indeed, the conduct of war and diplomacy was largely dependent on economic foundations.

Internal considerations were particularly important for France during the run up to the Second World War. Her leaders were constrained by the demographic consequences of the First World War and the economic consequences of the depression (which lifted later in France than elsewhere). The Left-wing Popular Front government, which had held power in 1936 and 1937, had sought to unite the country against Fascism and to speed up rearmament, but in practice the strikes that had accompanied this government had divided the country. Also, new social measures, such as the forty-hour week, were widely believed to have impeded rearmament. Considerations of internal politics also encouraged the French to put their faith in the Maginot line (the defensive fortifications along the eastern border). Historians have derided this strategy and pointed out how easily Hitler's tanks outflanked the Maginot line in 1940. But a defensive strategy made sense in terms of French internal politics. Firstly, France needed to protect her frontiers, rather than risk a mobile war, because so many of the natural resources that were perceived as essential to modern war were located close to the eastern frontier. Secondly, many in France feared that war on French soil would stimulate revolution; indeed, it was this fear that made General Weygand insist that the French sought an armistice after the German invasion of 1940. Thirdly, the Maginot line had been enormously expensive and it was difficult to accept that this expenditure had been in vain – furthermore expenditure on the line often benefited Alsace-Lorraine which, having been returned from Germany in 1919, was a politically sensitive region. Fourthly, defensive warfare was seen as part of the republican tradition. Offensive warfare was associated with authoritarian governments, and Charles de Gaulle linked his proposals for offensive tank-based warfare with the need for a professional army which was also seen as a threat to the republican tradition of the 'Nation in arms'.

Historians who condemn the leaders of the Western powers in the late 1930s should also look at the men who proposed more aggressive options. Winston Churchill had been raised to almost legendary status in England after 1945, but before the war he was regarded as an aging drunk with a reputation for theatrical gestures. His name was associated with atrocities (Tonypandy), disasters (Gallipoli) and party disloyalty. Paul Reynaud, a most prominent advocate of aggressive resistance to Hitler in France, did not have a much better reputation. He was a deeply patriotic man, but he had a gift for making enemies, and he had alienated much of the French bourgeoisie through his support for devaluation in the early 1930s.

Finally, and perhaps most importantly, it needs to be remembered that Germany seemed strong in Europe because she was the only purely European power in 1939. British statesmen were desperately concerned to maintain the resources to protect their sprawling empire. Indeed now some right-wingers, such as Alan Clark, argue that the ultimate destruction of the British Empire was an excessively high price for resisting Hitler in Europe. The French also had a large empire, and the knowledge that they could fall back on this empire made some French people more willing to accept the humiliating armistice that was signed with the Germans in 1940; Charles de Gaulle argued that empire should be used as a basis for resistance rather than a consolation and his struggle against the Vichy government was conducted largely in Africa. Even Spain had extra-European possessions. The Spanish Civil War, fought by battle hardened 'africanista' officers whose most effective troops were often Moroccans, was as much about Africa as about any European conflict; Franco's generals did much to keep out of the Second World War because they knew that an army designed for imperial police duties would not fare well against European armies. Mussolini confined his ambitions for conquest mainly to Abyssinia during the 1930s and only entered the European war in 1940 when he believed, mistakenly, that it was almost over.

Paul Preston
The Spanish Civil War: Right versus Left in the 1930s

The international context of the Spanish Civil War, and especially the support of the fascist powers for Franco, was of major importance in the outcome of the war. However, it is also important to understand the distinctively Spanish circumstances in which the war arose.

The central problem in looking at the Spanish Civil War is to disentangle its two contradictory but totally entwined natures. The Spanish Civil War is on the one hand very much a Spanish war. Twenty years ago, it was still a commonplace that it was a war between fascism and communism. Research into the agrarian origins of the Spanish Civil War and the various social conflicts in Spain that erupted in 1936 has suggested that the standard view was nonsense and that effectively the Spanish Civil War was many different kinds of war but fundamentally a Spanish war. However, it is impossible to ignore the extent to which the Spanish Civil War was almost equally an international war.

To approach the 'Spanishness' of the Spanish Civil War, it is essential to disentangle its long-term structural origins. In the 100 years prior to 1931, when the Second Republic was founded in Spain, it is possible to see a very clear division of the country into two hostile blocks. However in 1931 when the Second Republic was established no one, except a tiny minority of the lunatic fringe on the extreme right or left, believed that Spain's problems could be resolved only by war. Yet five years and three months later, in the summer of 1936, large numbers of people thought war was inevitable, and quite a lot of people actually thought it was desirable. Accordingly, as well as examining the long-term structural conflicts, it is also crucial to understand the day-to-day politics of the second Republic. A situation in 1931 in which the coming of the Republic was greeted by dancing in the street and popular acclaim, popular fiesta, was transformed by 1936 to such an extent that many Spaniards gloomily accepted that war was inevitable. The structural and conjunctural factors cannot be separated since the deep structural problems, conflicts and tensions were worked out in daily politics in the course of those five years.

An entirely different question to those concerning the coming of the war is 'Why did Franco win the Spanish Civil War?' The origins of the war are to be found in the social and political history of Spain. Its outcome resides largely in international diplomacy. Indeed the fate of the Spanish Republic can only be fully understood if the Spanish Civil War is seen not as a narrow, Spanish war, but rather as the last battle in a European civil war which had been going on since 1917.

The structural conflicts of pre-1931 Spain

In the nineteenth century, Spain was a fundamentally agrarian country. It had patches of advanced industry, steel and shipbuilding in the Basque country, coal mines in Asturias, textiles and chemical industries in Catalonia. But even more than Italy, Spain was a country of massively uneven growth and real political power was in the hands of the landowners. There was a kind of partnership between, on the one hand, what one might call the financial, industrial and mercantile bourgeoisie, which was relatively weak, and on the other hand, the really dominant force in the economy, the big landowners. The landowners tended to rule over enormous estates, or *latifundios*, which were worked by landless labourers who were totally vulnerable to the economic vagaries of the day. The landlords maintained a great reserve army of landless labour and so were successful in preventing the formation of unions and so on. It was the landowners who dominated national politics.

The political system in Spain between the 1870s and 1923 when this system finally broke down into a military dictatorship was one based on two great pillars, electoral falsification and physical violence. The system of electoral falsification rested above all on the fact that the social power of the landlords was such that they could guarantee the votes, where necessary, of those who worked for them. Sometimes it would not work, and it would be necessary to rig elections, with irregularities committed such as registering the dead in the local cemetery to vote. This system guaranteed that between 1876 and 1923, no government ever lost an election in Spain. Basically what would happen was that every four years one government would make way for another and the incoming government would organise the elections. The way in which governments could guarantee victory was shown very obviously in the fact that occasionally over-zealous electoral officials would announce election results a few days before the election had actually taken place, or there were also occasions on which very zealous local officials would ensure that the desired candidate won by as much as 115% of the vote.

The consequence was, at a very superficial level, political stability, but beneath it tremendous social instability, because nothing ever really changed. The two great parties of the day were called the

Conservatives and the Liberals, the idea being to emulate what was seen as Britain's democratic system. Those parties were simply branches of the landowning oligarchy. The Liberals really represented above all else the interests of the wheat-growers of the centre; the Conservatives largely represented above all else the interests of the fruit and wine producers of the south. Elections changed virtually nothing. Only a relatively small proportion of the electorate had the right to vote, and since nothing changed, the population was forced into apathy or violent opposition to the system. A very obvious illustration of this is a story told of the local political boss of a town in the province of Granada, who on one occasion was waiting for election results to arrive. When they arrived he read them and exclaimed:

> Who on earth would have believed this, we were absolutely convinced that we the Liberals were going to win these elections, and God has willed otherwise. It turns out that we the Conservatives have won.

Preventive brutality

It was at the moments of greatest social tension, when there were rural uprisings, strikes and so on, that the other arm of the system came into play, which was physical violence. The system was dependent on the presence of the army, and, in rural areas, of a virtual army of occupation which was the Civil Guard. The Civil Guard ruled over rural Spain, protecting the big estates from a rebellious peasantry by means of what one American sociologist terms 'preventive brutality'. A story which illustrates preventive brutality concerns a Civil Guard post in a particularly remote part of rural Spain. The garrison received a telegram which said:

> Seismic movement expected your province STOP Epicentre your station STOP Report immediately STOP

Three weeks later the Civil Guard HQ in Madrid received a telegram back which said:

> Seismic movement totally repressed STOP Epicentre arrested with forty accomplices STOP After torture and interrogation all have confessed and been shot STOP Regret delay in reply there was an earthquake here last week.

The impact of the First World War

It was a system in which violence was part of daily life. Now all this was changed dramatically in the course of the First World War. In the Great War Spain was neutral, and underwent a massive economic takeoff as a result of being able to export to both sides. There was a boom in agriculture, in the textile industry, in coal-mining and in the Basque shipbuilding industry. The consequences were, however, that although Spain did not, like say Italy or even Germany, undergo the terrible consequences of the war in terms of the killing and maiming of its people, it did in fact undergo massive social dislocation. The frenzy of exports meant that there were shortages and inflation. Working-class living standards went down, with indices of a drop in the consumption of basic foodstuffs, and this led to an increase in working-class militancy. It also, curiously, led to a kind of internal squabble among the ruling classes.

In an odd way, when the tensions reached crisis point in 1917, Spain experienced what in British history had taken place in 1832. In other words, the financial, industrial and mercantile bourgeoisie began to flex its muscles and to protest against the fact that political power was the monopoly of the landed obligarchy. In 1917 there was a brief alliance of circumstance between the political representatives of big business and the leaders of trade unions, in protest against what they saw as a corrupt political system. The system could not cope with the fact that Spain was being brought hurtling into the twentieth century as a result of the economic changes caused by the First World War. What in fact happened was that when, in order to back the reform movement of 1917, strikes broke out, the government very skilfully used the army to put down the strikes and then faced the industrialists with a challenge. Needless to say the bankers and industrialists decided they would rather stay in alliance with the landed oligarchy than risk their existence in what looked as though might turn into a genuinely revolutionary crisis.

The consequence of this was that, by 1918 when a great government of National Coalition was formed which linked the two great parties of the industrial and banking bourgeoisie, the two sides that would fight the Spanish Civil War were discernible. On the one hand, for all their divisions into socialists, anarcho-syndicalists, and very shortly communists too, there was the urban and rural proletariat. On the other side there was the industrial and financial bourgeoisie. Of course this is far too simple. To understand why the Second Republic broke down, it is crucial to add to the analysis an entire social class which, at least in the English-language historiography of this period, tends to be forgotten about.

The Catholic peasantry

It was during the First World War that 2 to 2.5 million Catholic smallholding peasants, mainly from central and northern Spain, entered the political arena. In the course of the First World War, a number of very far-sighted, progressive right-wingers had begun to fear the consequences of the spread in Spain of international ideologies like socialism and anarcho-syndicalism. They had concluded that the industrial proletariat was a lost cause, having already gone over to the left. However, they began a massive campaign during the First World War years to stop the rot spreading to the smallholding peasantry. In this they were helped by the fact that although the smallholders in question were very poor, and although their material interests might have been seen to lie with the left, all of the branches of the left, socialists, anarchists, and later communists, tended to despise them. The left believed that the future lay in collective agriculture and massive industrialisation. The extremely conservative smallholders, who were deeply attached to their own bit of land, were seen as a reactionary irrelevance. Therefore the left never did anything to try to recruit this very important social class.

The right on the other hand, during the First World War years, organised, in every province, a Catholic Agrarian Federation, which provided credit facilities, collectives to provide access to machinery, grain-warehousing and other services for the smallholding peasants. Attached was an ideological exigency which demanded that they reject socialist anarchism, which Catholic smallholders did willingly. In central and northern Spain, the Catholic Agrarian Federations were immensely successful in recruiting large numbers of Catholic peasants. They were to become the crucial electoral force of the right during the Second Republic. Curiously, although this is a slightly minor point, many Spanish volunteers, as opposed to foreign mercenaries who fought for Franco during the Spanish Civil War, were recruited from among those very same smallholding Catholics.

Accordingly, another factor may be added to the simple pattern that is emerging by 1918, with the two sides: the urban and rural proletariat, with all its internecine divisions, and the wealthy oligarchies of the land, banking and industry. What is going to make both the politics of the Second Republic work in the way they do and the Spanish Civil War be fought in the way it is, is the inclusion among the forces of the right of a huge constituency of smallholding farmers.

Primo de Rivera's dictatorship

Between 1918 and 1923, it became increasingly apparent that the old system based on the two pillars of electoral falsification and physical repression was finished. There was virtually a civil war in the south of Spain during this period, there was enormous physical violence and political gangsterism in the industrial towns of the north and, eventually to save the system, in 1923 a military dictatorship was imposed by General Miguel Primo de Rivera. His regime began all kinds of infrastructural schemes for railways, roads and electrification, ran up massive foreign debts, and when the Wall Street Crash came Spain was in a terrible mess. In numerous ways, he managed to offend most of his supporters, including the big landowners because of his paternalist policies, and the army by efforts to streamline promotion procedures. Finally, by 1930, it became apparent to him that he did not have the support of the army, nor indeed of the bulk of the population, and so he resigned.

With the resignation of Primo de Rivera, Spain faced a situation of great tension and latent conflict. A military dictatorship that had been brought in to save society failed, when everywhere else in Europe dictatorships were still being erected. The Spanish right saw the solution to its problems in authoritarian structures, and yet the dictatorship collapsed. Thus, for a brief moment, the idea of dictatorship as the solution to left-wing threats failed, and it was that which made possible the foundation of the Second Republic without violence. The right was in no position to fight to hold back the coming of democracy because, in the short term, there was nothing to put in its place. Within months of the Republic being established, of course, there were nostalgic glances back at the dictatorship as a great golden age and dreams about the establishment of a more durable dictatorship which would in the end be the Franco dictatorship. However, the important thing to remember is that the municipal elections of April 1931 which brought in the Second Republic were allowed to run to their conclusion, because the right, for a brief moment, felt itself bereft of weapons and tactics.

The Second Republic

The Second Republic was established, its government dominated by two major forces of the left and centre-left, the Socialist Party and a number of middle-class republican parties. They began to introduce a whole series of measures aimed at ameliorating the appalling living conditions of ordinary people in Spain. In doing so, they ensured that Spain's great underlying social conflicts were transmitted into national politics. The interests of the landless labourers were taken on board by the Socialist Party; those of the big landowners by the various parties of the right. The electoral victory in the spring of 1931 of the Republican-Socialist coalition brought a Socialist Minister of Labour, Francisco Largo Caballero.

En masse, landless labourers began to flood into the Socialist Landworkers Union, the FNTT. The FNTT was part of the biggest union in Spain, the Socialist UGT, the General Union of Labour. Before 1931, only something like 17% of its membership were peasants. By the end of 1931 nearly 40% of its members were landless labourers.

The UGT was intimately connected with the Socialist Party, much more closely than the Labour Party and the TUC have ever been. Accordingly, its biggest bloc of support came from landless labourers. Its second biggest section was constituted by mineworkers. In the Depression, Spanish mining was going through a deep crisis. Agriculture and mining were the two areas where, at a local level, social conflict was most vicious with daily violence on a scale which is difficult to imagine. When the Socialist Party came into power, it introduced various reforms which were meant merely to make life easier for the landless peasant. In fact in a context of international depression, they had the consequence of totally challenging the entire economic system. The package consisted of, for instance, the introduction of the eight-hour day for rural workers, in a context in which previously workers had worked from sun-up to sun-down, which meant that they might do a 16-hour day. In order for the law to be applied, the owner either had to employ twice the number of workers to do the same work, or pay the existing workers double the salary. That was a serious blow to the economy of the big estates at a time when they were unable to pass on these costs by exporting.

The right under threat

Equally dramatic in its impact was the so-called Degree of Obligatory Cultivation. It ensured that any land which had been used for agrarian cultivation should remain so. It aimed to stop the big landowners using their greatest weapon against the left, which was the rural lockout. Similarly, the Decree of Municipal Boundaries stated that, within a given municipality, no new labour could be employed until everyone who was resident within that municipality had found work. Another one of the great weapons of the big landowners at harvest time was to bring in cheap labour from outside the area to keep wages down and to prevent the local workers uniting to try and push up wages. Inevitably the right was outraged by what it saw as this challenge, and it found two ways of defending itself. One can be described as the legalist way, creating a political party, which at first was called Popular Action, and from 1933, the CEDA. This was a Catholic authoritarian party, which was successful precisely because it was able to count on the votes of the Catholic smallholders who had been attracted in the First World War period to the right-wing cause. However, there were those on the right who were not satisfied with this legalist defence of right-wing interests and they adopted what was called the catastrophist solution. They believed that the only real defence of right-wing interests was to destroy the Republic in a great catastrophe and bring in a new dictatorship. In a sense theirs was the scenario for what actually happened in 1936. The catastrophists consisted of various monarchist factions and the Spanish Fascist Party, the Falange.

In 1933, the left-wing coalition in Spain split up in frustration at the fact that the right had been very successful in blocking reform at the local level. The right won the elections of 1933, and totally polarised Spanish politics by the rapid abolition of most of the reforms that had been introduced in the previous two years. It is worth noting that the Spanish electoral system at this time ensured that a tiny swing in the number of votes cast at an election led to a huge swing in the number of seats held in the Cortes. Although, in the 1933 elections, there was only a relatively small swing of votes from the left to the right, parliamentary power swung dramatically. The same was to happen again in 1936 with the election of the Popular Front. Part of the answer to the question, why did the Second Republic break down, lies in the electoral mechanisms of the time, which ensured a destabilising pendulum effect every time there was an election. The right governed for two years, which came to be called the two black years, because they abolished the social legislation of the first two years. The consequent increase in social tension erupted into a miners' uprising in October 1934 which was put down by the army. That fact finally had a major impact on the minds of supporters of both the right and left. On the left, people realised that they had to unite in order to gain political power, to prevent a return to the right. Those on the right drew the conclusion from the left's reunification that even the political power they had won by electoral means was always vulnerable. There could always be other elections, with a united left voting against them. Therefore, it made much more sense to plan for a civil war and the imposition of a dictatorship. Although some elements had been planning since the first day of the Republic to overthrow it, serious planning began in 1936. The catastrophists were right. At the end of 1935, the right-wing government had fallen. In February 1936 there were elections which the left, reunited as the Popular Front, won. A small swing in the popular vote led to a great shift in power in Parliament to the parties of the left. After the experience of 1933–1935 the left was determined not to be swindled out of their social reforms as they felt they had been after the first two years. For its part the right began to put all of its efforts into mounting a military conspiracy.

Military uprising

The Second Republic broke down because the unresolved social conflicts of pre-1931 were transmitted into day-to-day politics. What then happened was a military uprising. In part, the coup was to put a stop to the challenges to the right-wing landed interests. The mentality of Spanish army officers, however, was such that one of the things they most deeply resented about the Second Republic was that it had introduced regional devolution. Spanish army officers, not having won any major battles in the previous 100 years, were determined that the one battle they would win was the battle to keep Spain united.

That military coup should have been defeated quite easily. The conspirators' idea was that, in each of the 50 provinces of Spain, a military garrison would rise up and it would successfully establish its authority. It would have a black list of those on the left who needed to be shot, and perhaps within a couple of weeks a military dictatorship would be established. What happened, to the surprise of many of the officers, is that in those parts of Spain, either the deep south where the landless labourers were the majority, or in the big industrial towns like Madrid and Barcelona where there was a strong working class, the workers seized arms and took upon themselves the job of fighting off the military coup. The consequence was that, one week after the military coup had taken place, it had been successful in exactly those places where there were Catholic small-holding peasants who had voted for the parties of the right during the Republic. In those other areas of big industrial towns and big estates the left dominated. What was meant to be a quick coup left Spain geographically and politically divided for a lengthy war. Equally, the Republic was divided between the conventional bourgeois government and the revolutionary aspirations of the workers.

Had the Spanish Civil War remained a Spanish war, it is a reasonable speculation that the war would have been won by the Republic. In fact the army was divided; only a part of the officer corps rose up against the Republic, especially the officers who had served in Morocco. Most of the very senior officers stayed loyal to the Republic. It was the young colonels and the majors who were most prominent in the rising. The most important section of the Spanish army was to be found in Morocco. The Spanish Moroccan army were brutal, ruthless and the only battle-hardened element of the army. However, the Straits of Gibraltar were in the hands of the Republic because the Navy had mutinied and Republican sailors had taken it over. What turned a military coup that was going very badly wrong, into a long-term civil war, and in fact an international civil war, was the intervention of Hitler.

The international dimension

It was the fact that Hitler responded to Franco's pleas for help and provided the transport planes that got the Spanish Moroccan army across the Straits and into Spain, that kept Franco in the game. It was also a major contributing factor to why Franco won the Spanish Civil War. The other factor, and an enormously complex one, is the fact that the democracies, Britain and France, refused help to the Republic. They acted in this way because they were suspicious that the Republic was too left-wing, because they did not want to risk a general war, because they had an ambiguous attitude to Hitler and they were attracted by the idea that they would use Hitler to crush the left in Spain and elsewhere in Europe. The fact that Britain and France refused to help the Spanish Republic threw the government into the arms of the Soviet Union which was the only major power that was prepared to help. Unfortunately for the Spanish Republic, Soviet foreign policy was, as might be expected, conducted in the interests of the Soviet Union. The Soviet Union, because of its perception of the long-term threat of Hitler, was keen to establish an alliance with France, the traditional ambition of Soviet foreign policy to encircle Germany. The USSR was therefore anxious not to offend Britain and France by seeming to foster revolution in Spain. The long-term interests of Russian foreign policy ensured that Soviet aid to the Spanish Republic would be conditional upon the crushing of the revolution.

The revolution which had broken out when the workers seized arms to oppose the military coup, had aroused enormous popular enthusiasm. In a sense, the greatest weapon that the Spanish Republic had was that popular enthusiasm. Its annihilation was the price charged by the Soviet Union for its aid. That, and Spain's gold reserves. Thus, the domestic problems of the Spanish Republic inevitably became entangled with the international context. That context, the abandoning of the Republic by the democracies, the forced reliance on the Soviet Union, led inexorably to massive demoralisation within the Republican zone. Faced with the united Franco force backed by the unstinting help of Hitler and Mussolini, the defeat of the Second Republic seems in retrospect inevitable.

Paul Preston is Professor of International History at the London School of Economics.

Richard Cockett
Appeasement: Britain's Prime Minister in the Dock

Richard Cockett considers some arguments in defence of appeasement before coming down firmly on the other side.

It seems to be the fate of certain British statesmen to be inextricably bound to a place-name in the popular imagination. Just as the name of Eden, for all his other achievements, conjures up the demon of Suez, so the name of Churchill, after but a moment's reflection, will similarly induce the ghost of Gallipoli – which remained to haunt him for the rest of his career.

But at least it could be said that they went down fighting! The same cannot be said of the two British Prime Ministers whose names will always be indelibly associated with the two great cities of Germany, from where they both brought back 'Peace with honour' – Disraeli from Berlin in 1878 and Neville Chamberlain from Munich in 1938. Although Disraeli made no such prediction, he also brought back peace in his time (for the subsequent 36 years); it was Chamberlain's misfortune to claim peace in *his* time and yet to be at war within a year. For this Chamberlain has been as vilified as any figure in British history. Indeed, the literature denigrating Chamberlain and the Munich Agreement is now almost as great as the literature in praise of Chamberlain and the Munich conference at the time.

However, we are now, through the possession of all the relevant contemporary documents, both British and European, able to come to some dispassionate conclusions as to why Chamberlain had to endure that most wretched year, from triumph in September 1938 to despair in September 1939. The failure of his policy lay as much with Chamberlain's predecessors as it did with him, but the failings of his predecessors were compounded by Chamberlain's own shortcomings as a statesman which ultimately blinded him to the realities confronting him as Prime Minister from 1937 to 1940.

The 'Slave Treaty' of Versailles

To understand Chamberlain's foreign policy and why it failed, it is important first of all to understand what Chamberlain was trying to achieve. Chamberlain was never in any doubt as to his broad aim. As he told the House of Commons in December 1937: 'We have a definite objective in front of us. That objective is a general settle-ment of the grievances of the world without war.' The grievances of which he spoke arose, of course, out of the Treaty of Versailles that had redrawn the map of Europe in the wake of the First World War. To the victorious powers of the First World War – namely Britain and France – it was a peace settlement, but to the Germans it was a diktat, the dictated, imposed settlement forced upon them by deceit and against their will. They had come to Versailles to negotiate freely, and left as slaves. That much was felt by all Germans and quickly came to be felt by all thinking English people and French people as well. Germany had considered that it was going to negotiate on the basis of President Wilson's fourteen points, but the sole point of the eventual peace treaty seemed to be to disarm and dismember Germany to such an extent that she was not only no longer a 'Great Power', but scarcely a 'power' at all. The majority of Allied politicians at Versailles seem to have been guided by motives of revenge against the German-speaking peoples for the sins of their history rather than a sense of the need for positive European reconstruction in the future. This post-1919 status quo in Europe, therefore, was one that no German could consider with equanimity. A. J. P. Taylor in *The Origins of the Second World War*, published in 1974, correctly observed that for the Germans:

> . . . the status quo was not peace, but a slave treaty . . . the vanquished power wanted to undo its defeat. This latter ambition, whether 'aggressive' or not, was not peculiar to Hitler. It was shared by all German politicians, by the Social Democrats who ended the war in 1918 as much as by Stresemann.

Indeed, the minute that the ink was dry on the treaty, the Germans started work to undo or circumvent the terms of Ver-sailles. Stresemann, the great foreign minister of the Weimar Republic from 1923 to 1929, privately admitted in 1925 that his ambition was to achieve 'the readjustment of our eastern frontiers; the recovery of Danzig, the Polish corridor'. In 1926 the Treaty of Berlin was signed between Germany and Russia offering the German forces an opportunity to develop prohibited weapons and to rearm on Russian soil. Hitler, who came to power in 1933, was not altering German policy in his desire to revise totally the Versailles settlement, he was merely committed to pursuing that policy in a much more vigorous and dangerous fashion.

The aims of the appeasers

If German politicians were motivated by a feeling of dishonour and thus revenge in the post-Versailles world, British politicians tended to be motivated by feelings of guilt for a treaty that most came to see as unfair and unworkable. Amongst those who shared this sentiment were most of that generation of Conservative politicians who rose to direct British policy in the 1930s. Steeped in their reading of J. M. Keynes's classic denunciation of Versailles, *The Economic Consequences of the Peace*, this generation recognised that Versailles had been, by and large, a mistake and that unless treaty revision was undertaken, a resentful, embittered but not necessarily weak Germany would seek to do that job herself. These politicians were liberal Conservatives: they were progressive politicians who sought to act morally and to work for change if that change were desirable. They were motivated by the spirit of the bible of liberal Toryism, Peel's *Tamworth Manifesto*, which in 1835 had committed the modern Conservative to be neither the 'defender of abuses' nor the 'enemy of judicious reforms'. The men who conducted the policy of appeasement were liberal Conservatives, concerned with reform at home *and* abroad.

Lord Halifax, Chamberlain's Foreign Secretary from 1938 to 1940, had written *The Great Opportunity* with George Lloyd in 1919 which had become the beacon for that generation of aspiring Tories who looked to a better postwar world than that which seemed to be contemplated by their elders. He was instrumental, as Viceroy of India from 1925 to 1931, in putting India on the road to self-government and in convening the London round-table conference on India in 1931 which was attended by Gandhi. Halifax had been helped in this task by Sir Samuel Hoare who, as Secretary of State for India from 1931 to 1935, was responsible for furthering Indian progress towards self-government: Hoare was also a reforming Home Secretary from 1937 to 1939 with a particular interest in penal reform. Stanley Baldwin's main concern had been to solve industrial strife at home, and had successfully healed the wounds of the General Strike of 1926 by the time that he was called upon to preside over the liberal option of the abdication of Edward VIII in 1936. Lord Astor, whose paper *The Observer* was an early supporter of treaty revision, was dedicated to agriculture and health reform. Chamberlain himself had made his name as a pioneering Minister of Health from 1924 to 1929 in Baldwin's Cabinet. The youngest government appeaser and Under-Secretary at the Foreign Office under Halifax from 1938 to 1940 was R. A. Butler who went on to become the standard-bearer of postwar progressive Conservatism and the author of the *Industrial Charter* of 1947, the blueprint for the consensus politics of the Welfare State that prevailed in Britain up to 1979. He was motivated by the same spirit of improvement and reform as Halifax, Baldwin, Hoare and Chamberlain himself. The Treaty of Versailles was obviously an 'abuse', both in practical and moral terms, and was thus doubtlessly susceptible to 'judicious reform'.

The principles that guided these politicians in their activities in domestic affairs thus guided their approach to foreign affairs. Furthermore, they recognised that to defend the Versailles settlement en masse was just as bad as attempting to change it by force. The high priest of appeasement, E. H. Carr, wrote of this general predicament in his review of foreign policy during the interwar years, *The Twenty Years Crisis*, published in 1939:

> The defence of the status quo is not a policy which can be lastingly successful. It will end in war as surely as rigid conservatism will end in revolution. 'Resistance to aggression', however necessary as a momentary device of national policy, is no solution, for readiness to fight to prevent change is just as immoral as readiness to fight to enforce it.

The policy adopted by the British politicians towards the Treaty of Versailles in the postwar world was thus one of 'judicious reform'. Appeasement was a policy designed to alter the status quo peacefully by meeting German grievances. A. J. P. Taylor has written that:

> Appeasement had been in origin a high-minded attempt at the impartial redress of grievances . . . Chamberlain . . . was confident that his programme would work. His motive throughout was the general pacification of Europe. He was driven on by hope, not fear. It did not occur to him that Great Britain and France were unable to oppose German demands; rather he assumed that Germany, and Hitler in particular, would be grateful for concessions willingly made.

That the Versailles treaty was riddled with 'abuses' was never questioned. Throughout the course of the late 1930s Chamberlain was to be confronted by the dilemma of whether to stand by those artificial creations of Versailles, such as Austria and Czechoslovakia, which he knew to be largely unworkable, or follow his own 'appeasing' instincts and let them dissolve. Why should Britain stand in the way of the German minority of 3¼ million in Czechoslovakia returning to Germany from whence they had been plucked at the whim of some anonymous Versailles negotiator in 1919? Surely the rights of self-determination dictated that these Sudeten Germans should have the right to return to Germany, and the same in Austria and Danzig? Basil Newton, Britain's Minister in Prague, echoed Chamberlain's thoughts exactly when he wrote to the

Foreign Office in March 1938 that Czechoslovakia's position, as then constituted, was 'not permanently tenable', and the most that Britain and France could do by going to war over it would be 'to restore after a lengthy struggle a status quo which had already proved unacceptable and which, even if restored, would probably again prove unworkable'.

Furthermore, Chamberlain and his colleagues also believed that a revision of the Treaty of Versailles, whereby the German people in Austria, Poland and Czechoslovakia were united once again, would not prejudice British interests, and might even help those interests. Sir Nevile Henderson, Britain's Ambassador in Berlin and an arch-appeaser, put the case well when he wrote to Halifax in March 1939:

> Hitler made it very clear in *Mein Kampf* that *Lebensraum* for Germany could only be found in expansion eastwards, and expansion eastwards renders a clash between Germany and Russia some day or other highly probable. With a benevolent Britain on her flank, Germany can envisage such an eventuality with comparative equanimity . . . The best approach to good relations with Germany is therefore along the lines of the avoidance of constant and vexatious interference in matters in which British interests are not directly or vitally involved . . .

Even those who stood by Britain's traditional policy of maintaining a balance of power in Europe found it hard to contemplate British intervention in that part of Europe that was essentially Germany's 'backyard'. As Chamberlain famously broadcast on September 27 1937, with the prospect of war looming in front of him, it was indeed 'horrible, fantastic, incredible' that Londoners should be 'digging ditches and trying on gas masks here because of a quarrel in a far-away country between people of whom we know nothing.'

The problem of appeasement

So the conundrum of appeasement is this. How did Chamberlain and Hitler drift into war when they were largely motivated by the same concern for the revision of the European status quo? The answer lies both in the chronology of events and the unbending, inflexible character of the British Prime Minister. E. H. Carr was already clutching at this point only weeks after Britain declared war on Germany on 3 September 1939:

> In March 1939, the Prime Minister admitted that in all the modifications of the treaty down to and including the Munich Agreement, there was 'something to be said' for the necessity of

change in the existing situation. If, in 1935 and 1936, this 'something' had been clearly and decisively said, to the exclusion of scolding and protests, by the official spokesman of the status quo powers it might not yet have been too late to bring further changes within the framework of peaceful negotiation. The tragedy by which successive removals of long recognised injustices of the Versailles Treaty became a cause not of reconciliation, but of further estrangement, between Germany and the Versailles Powers, and destroyed instead of increasing the limited stock of common feeling which had formerly existed, is one for which the sole responsibility cannot be laid at Germany's door.

There is a great deal of truth in this. Two Foreign Office officials most linked with Whitehall opposition to appeasement, Sir Orme Sargent and Ralph Wigram, had warned in a memorandum of November 1935 that 'the ex-Allied powers should come to terms with Germany in order to remove grievances by friendly arrangement and by the process of give and take, *before Germany once again takes the law into her own hands* [my italics].' Essentially, what Chamberlain was doing was implementing the right policy several years too late, for by the time Chamberlain was putting out his first diplomatic feeler to Hitler vis-à-vis his cherished European settlement with Lord Halifax's visit to Berlin in November 1937, Hitler had already decided that the 'hate-inspired' and 'satiated' British Empire would never tolerate the middle European German hegemony that he had in mind. The meeting that Hitler held with his Chiefs of Staff that has now passed into history as the Hossbach Memorandum, outlining Hitler's plans for the 'acquisition' of Austria and Czechoslovakia, had already taken place two weeks before Halifax arrived in Germany. In January 1938, Ribbentrop, the German ambassador to London and a close ideological ally of Hitler, warned that no settlement with Britain was possible, so Germany's task was now to 'foster England's belief that a settlement . . . between England and Germany [was] still possible eventually' as this 'might, for example, have a restraining effect on any possible intention to intervene on the part of the British government, should Germany become involved in a local conflict in Central Europe'. In other words, from the very moment that Chamberlain began to pursue appeasement positively, Berlin was prepared to string him along for any short-term tactical advantage it could gain, having already discounted the general European settlement that Chamberlain was pursuing.

The plain fact was that Hitler had been appointed Chancellor in 1933 and commanded the will and assent of German people precisely because he stood for a dynamic revision of the Versailles settlement, which his Weimar predecessors had been unable to deliver. By 1936, when Hitler started his unilateral, military revision of Versailles by marching into the Rhineland, Germany had gained nothing – bar Locarno and the Anglo-German Naval Treaty – by waiting on the Allies to take the initiative on treaty revision. As Wigram and Sargent had warned, by the time that Chamberlain came to power in May 1937, Hitler was thus prepared to 'take the law into his own hands'. By the time that Chamberlain tried boldly to seize the initiative in November 1937 it was too late; Hitler had risen to pre-eminence in Germany because the Germans had failed to gain anything by the process of 'judicious reform' that the embattled MacDonald and supine Baldwin had only chatted about and which Chamberlain eventually tried to act on. Chamberlain's predecessors – namely Baldwin and MacDonald – might have accepted the principles of appeasement, but they had done absolutely nothing about putting those principles into practice. Their foreign policy, although that word itself suggests a firmness of purpose that neither premier possessed, was essentially one of drift. They had neither applied themselves to the cause of treaty revision nor had they stood by the obligations imposed upon them by the existing treaties, and it was left to the unfortunate Chamberlain to try and rescue British policy from this unhappy legacy of drift and compromise. Chamberlain's initiative was too little, far too late. If Chamberlain had been Prime Minister in 1925 and offered a similar initiative to Stresemann, Hitler would probably never have *needed* to come to power.

The failure of Chamberlain

Chamberlain never appreciated this. His laudable idea for a general European settlement based on the removal of German grievances had become an *idée fixe* even before Halifax's first discouraging mission to Berlin in 1937. After that, Chamberlain refused to countenance anything that seemed to conflict with or undermine his policy. As one Conservative colleague observed, Chamberlain 'knew his own mind and saw to it that he had his own way. An autocrat with all the courage of his convictions right or wrong'. Having set his course, he would not be swayed; anyone who endeavoured to point out that Hitler was not amenable to 'judicious reform' was either dismissed, ignored or forced to resign – Sir Robert Vansittart, Churchill, Eden and Duff Cooper were only the most prominent of those who stood in Chamberlain's way and were made to pay for it. Chamberlain's inflexible resolve made him a formidable politician, but quite unable to respond to changing circumstances or fresh evidence that might have informed or even altered his policy. His response to criticism was to quash it, not to listen to it. At Munich he believed that he had won 'peace in our time', not at gunpoint but by the force of diplomatic persuasion. His capacity for self-delusion was quite extraordinary if it helped him to believe that his *idée fixe* was still valid and intact – but then that is the vice of strong-willed politicians.

Duff Cooper, the First Lord of the Admiralty, resigned from the Cabinet in the wake of Munich simply because he could not believe that the secession of the Sudetenland to Germany would bring 'peace in our time', and in this he was absolutely correct. All Munich did was to stimulate Hitler's already voracious territorial appetite. As Duff Cooper later wrote of Munich:

> If I thought surrender would bring lasting peace I should be in favour of surrender, but I did not believe there would ever be peace in Europe as long as Nazism ruled in Germany. The next act of aggression might be one that it would be far harder for us to resist.

That is the burden of the case against Munich in a nutshell. All that Chamberlain's appeasement did in practice was to swell Hitler's appetite for territorial annexation and strengthen his domestic political position, for nothing succeeded for him like success. Appeasement achieved exactly the opposite of what it had been designed to achieve. It is true that Hitler did not want a world war in 1939, but that was only because since 1936 he had come to expect a complete lack of resistance to any of his territorial acquisitions; he was certain that a 'local war' with Poland was possible without the intervention of either Britain or France. Arthur Mann, editor of the *Yorkshire Post*, argued quite correctly in a leader of 8 December 1938 that by 'repeatedly surrendering to force, [Chamberlain] has repeatedly encouraged aggression . . . our central contention, therefore, is that Mr Chamberlain's policy has throughout been based on a fatal misunderstanding of the psychology of dictatorship'. By the time that Hitler invaded Poland on 1 September 1939, confidently expecting the same British and French response to his invasion of the Rhineland, Austria, the Sudetenland and the rest of Czechoslovakia in March 1939, his press chief, Otto Dietrich, later observed that Hitler was 'like a roulette player who cannot quit the tables because he thinks he has a system that will break the bank'.

And with good reason.

Richard Cockett teaches History at Royal Holloway, University of London.

Patrick Condren
Soviet Foreign Policy 1917–1941

It is fair to say that all Soviet primary and secondary sources are, to varying degrees, suspect. To build up as accurate a picture as possible the researcher must use Soviet materials in conjunction with the relevant Western sources.

The study of the diplomacy of the interwar period is one which has been clouded by emotional judgements. For many in the West, especially on the left, the establishment of the Soviet regime seemed to represent the great hope for the future and for surprisingly many, disillusionment came only slowly. The wartime alliance with the USSR further added to a certain reluctance to see Soviet foreign policy making in a clear light. The inter-war economic crisis, the rise of fascism, Nazi and Japanese aggression and the failure of the policy of appeasement, aided by the undeniable successes of the Soviet propaganda machine, all helped to obscure the fact that from the first, the Soviet leadership pursued its aims with whatever means were at its disposal.

The aims of Soviet Foreign Policy

In November 1917 the new Bolshevik government seemed unlikely to survive and 24 years later, in the autumn of 1941, few contemporary observers expected the Stalinist dictatorship to last out the year. These two facts perhaps help to demonstrate that the primary foreign policy aim of the Soviet government throughout this period was survival in what was with some justice seen as a hostile world. The other aim, or hope, was that the world revolution predicted by Marx would take place soon and that if it did not, then the actions of the Comintern might help to bring it about. By the mid-twenties this seemed increasingly unlikely.

Methods

From the very outset the Soviet government adopted a high moral tone in its comments on international relations, claiming and frequently repeating that the uniquely progressive nature of the Soviet social and political system made it unlike any other regime and that therefore, in marked contrast to imperialist powers, the aims and principles on which it based its conduct of foreign affairs were open diplomacy, self-determination, disarmament and the peace of nations. Apart from anything else, this approach highlights one consistent method of Soviet foreign policy – the use of propaganda to appeal to the masses over the heads of their governments. But more importantly, as a study of the period will reveal, whatever its professed principles, the Soviet government was utterly unscrupulous in its conduct of foreign affairs. When it was weak, peace and disarmament were obviously sensible things to strive for in the public arena, while the USSR built up its strength. When collective security seemed likely to bear fruit, the USSR followed this policy. When the best guarantee of Soviet security was war and occupation, then these methods were used instead. Open diplomacy and national self-determination were no more than catch phrases to confuse the naive or unwary, and certainly the Ukrainians and Georgians were under no illusions with regard to the second point by 1922. Further confusion can be caused if one ignores the fact that the Soviet government was perfectly capable of following two apparently contradictory policies at the same time and, in fact, frequently did so.

How strong was the Soviet Union?

Perhaps the most important thing to grasp about this period is that the Soviet Union was not yet a 'superpower'. It is probably fair to say that the Soviet Union was not even a world power, except in the sense that its territory still covered a large part of the world's land surface. For most of the 24 years under discussion the Soviet Union was industrially backward and, variously, in the throes of civil war, famine, Stalin's forced economic revolution and his murderous purges. By the late 1930s the extraordinary achievements of the five year plans, whatever the human cost, had immeasurably strengthened the USSR industrially and militarily, but even then, most informed sources in the West realised that Stalin's purges of the armed forces had, for the moment, drastically undermined Soviet military potential, as the war with Finland demonstrated.

Despite this material weakness, the Soviet government's ideology undoubtedly inspired fear in her immediate neighbours and among the ruling circles of the major powers, especially in the early years after the October Revolution. This 'Red Scare' was no doubt useful to conservative forces in the West even when it was obvious that the USSR was virtually powerless. When the World Revolution failed to materialise, Soviet leaders realised that some form of accommodation had to be sought with the hostile bourgeois states which surrounded the USSR, but the public utterances retained their heavy Marxist-Leninist content whatever tactical move the Soviet government happened to be following at the time.

It was an article of faith with Soviet foreign policy experts that all imperialist powers were automatically hostile to the world's first socialist state. With the experience of Brest-Litovsk and Allied intervention during the civil war, as well as their ideological background, this is hardly surprising. Therefore if an alliance had to be made with a particular capitalist power, it was purely a question of expediency, not of sentiment, for in Soviet eyes fascism and democracy were just two different forms of the enemy, capitalism.

Who made Soviet Foreign Policy?

From the revolution until the late 1920s, foreign policy was made by the relevant People's Commissar in consultation with senior Politburo colleagues. Trotsky was the first People's Commissar for Foreign Affairs until 1918, when he was replaced by G. V. Chicherin who stayed in office until 1930. After this time, as in all other matters, it was Stalin whose decision was final, though it is not impossible that he let Maxim Litvinov have his head during his nine years in charge of the Narkomindel (People's Commissariat of Foreign Affairs) from 1930 to 1939, while Stalin himself took foreign policy initiatives which secretly contradicted the USSR's public position. The replacement (but not death or humiliation) of Litvinov by Stalin's old crony V. M. Molotov in May 1939 is generally taken to demonstrate Stalin's decision to 'play the German card' as the international crisis deepened.

Phase 1: October 1917 to March 1918

In this extraordinary period when the Bolsheviks were flushed with success, their behaviour in the international sphere was as deliberately provocative as possible. The Decree on Peace issued the day after the Bolshevik coup, plus the sensational publication of the Tsarist secret treaties and the repudiation of all legal ties with other nations made by the Tsarist regime, was the first foreign policy act of the new government. Neither Lenin nor Trotsky believed that they were going to 'have' foreign relations in the accepted sense and Trotsky assumed he could issue a few proclamations and then 'shut up shop'. The expectation that a world revolution was nigh led to the distinctly unconventional approach to the negotiations with the Germans at Brest-Litovsk. The troops of the Central Powers were bombarded with Bolshevik propaganda while the Soviet delegation wasted as much time as possible. After some months of this the Germans lost patience and forced the Bolsheviks to accept the savage treaty which deprived the old Russian Empire of so much of its territory, population and resources.

Phase 2: March 1918 to 1921

After Brest-Litovsk it was quite clear that not even the survival of the Soviet government could be taken for granted. Foreign affairs in the conventional sense hardly existed during the bitter fighting between the Reds and the many foreign supporters of the White armies during the civil war. For a while, the newly founded Comintern's hopes of a spreading proletarian revolution must have seemed high with, at various times, Bela Kun's brief success in Hungary, a Soviet government in Bavaria, the Spartakists in Berlin and numerous other disturbances across Europe, not to mention the Red Army's tantalisingly close approach to Warsaw in 1920.

By the end of the civil war, however, the reality of the Soviet international position was only too clear. Soviet Russia was economically devastated, militarily weak and, from a territorial point of view, separated from the more developed parts of Europe by a wall of hostile states ranging from Finland in the north,through Estonia, Latvia, Lithuania and Poland to a newly enlarged Rumania in the south. All communist insurrections had been crushed by the forces of reaction and to all intents and purposes Soviet Russia was little more than an irritant to the victorious Entente Powers who dominated early postwar Europe. Russia was excluded from the League of Nations and was not yet formally recognised by any major power. The most pressing problem for the Narkomindel was to secure something like normal diplomatic and economic relations with as many states as possible.

Phase 3: 1921 to c. 1931

The next decade saw the birth and development of the curious relationship between communist Russia and capitalist Weimar Germany which was the main plank of Soviet foreign policy until Hitler came to power in 1933. Negotiations between the two countries had been in progress since early 1921 and secret contacts had already been made in the diplomatic, commercial and military fields. The failure of the World Economic Conference at Genoa in 1922 had led the Soviet and German delegations to conclude the Treaty of Rapallo by which diplomatic and economic relations were established between the two 'outcast' countries. Within a few months secret military agreements were signed which led to the setting up on Soviet soil of joint German–Soviet training bases in the fields of aerial, armoured and chemical warfare. It is perhaps worth noting at this point that already by 1922 the Soviet authorities had left behind the idealistic concepts of open diplomacy and disarmament and that the 'twin track' approach of attempting to foment revolution in those countries with which the USSR had regular diplomatic relations was seen as normal.

The relationship with Germany was not untroubled. The Comintern's failed attempts to rekindle the German revolution in 1921 and 1923 were not helpful. The Narkomindel was greatly alarmed at Germany's *rapprochement* with the Entente Powers when she signed the Locarno agreements in 1925 and joined the League of Nations the year after. However, the Treaty of Berlin in 1926, which reaffirmed Rapallo, and important German–Soviet trade treaties in 1925 and 1931 demonstrated that both governments found their links much too valuable to let ideology or diplomatic manoeuvring get in the way.

As far as the rest of the world was concerned, the Soviet government enjoyed some limited success. Formal recognition by Great Britain in 1924 and by most other nations around this time at least made Soviet isolation less acute, but Soviet newspapers still gave the impression that the capitalist world was on the point of launching another intervention against the world's first workers' state. This somewhat paranoid approach fed off incidents like the 1927 rupture of diplomatic relations by Great Britain, and the Soviet press frequently described the League of Nations as little more than a thinly disguised conspiracy to attack the USSR. Even the Kellogg-Briand Pact of 1928 was vitually characterised as yet another attempt to undermine world peace! No doubt this atmosphere of hysteria was largely designed for internal consumption, especially as an extra stimulus to Stalin's economic revolution, but it did little to lessen the general distaste and suspicion felt towards the Soviet Union by most European governments.

In China the USSR suffered an important reverse when the Chinese Communist Party was dealt a savage blow by Chiang Kai Shek's massacre in Shanghai in 1927. This was also a blow to the Comintern policy of the 'united front from above' which hoped to strengthen the role of foreign communist parties by ordering them to support nationalists or other left-wing groups. The situation in the Far East was to prove the most worrying to Moscow as Japanese attitudes to China became increasingly aggressive.

As the 1920s came to an end the Soviet international position seemed far more encouraging than at any time since the revolution. The USSR had achieved international acceptance, her economic transformation was under way, she had a valuable working relationship with Germany and her skilful use of propaganda, such as Litvinov's 1927 demand for immediate and total disarmament at the Geneva Preparatory Commission on Disarmament, had given her a position of moral leadership for much of the world's left. Without doubt the most satisfying development was the economic catastrophe which hit the capitalist world in 1929. The political effects of this crisis were, however, to bring about a rapid readjustment of Moscow's policies.

Phase 4: c. 1931 to 1934

In this period the USSR managed to conclude a series of neutrality or non-aggression pacts with most of her neighbours. Probably the most significant were those made with Poland and France in 1932. Of largely symbolic importance, these pacts nonetheless publicly demonstrated the USSR's desire for peace, stability and international acceptance, and proved to be a vital preparation for the realignment of Soviet foreign policy that was begun by events in the Far East.

The Japanese attack on China in 1931 and the subsequent setting up of the huge puppet state of Manchukuo right on the Soviet Far Eastern border was an extremely alarming development for Stalin. It made further Japanese expansion into Siberia seem a distinct possibility and the lack of a firm French and British response to the Manchurian crisis, both within and outside the League, probably made Stalin suspicious of the West's intentions. A conspiracy of imperialist powers would always seem more plausible to Stalin as an explanation of Western actions than mere weakness or incompetence. Stalin soon pragmatically resumed relations with and arms deliveries to Chiang Kai Shek, and military strength in the Soviet Far East was steadily increased.

The situation was also changing in Europe. The collapse of rational politics in Germany as the economic crisis worsened was not at first the disaster it later became for Stalin. The Soviet interpretation of events in Germany was that the polarisation in politics could only ultimately lead to a strengthening of the KPD and that the Nazis' 'short-lived' success would presage some sort of left-wing revolution. As a result the KPD was ordered to attack the middle ground of German politics, labelling the SPD 'social fascists'. Stalin was not the only one to underestimate the power of Hitler and the Nazis. After a year of confused signals from Berlin, it became quite obvious in the Kremlin that the German link was no longer to be relied upon. Although economic relations continued, the secret military cooperation was ended by Hitler, the KPD was destroyed, the tone of the Nazi press was distinctly anti-Soviet, and the expansionist aims of Hitler's foreign policy were openly discussed.

Anxious at this deterioration in the USSR's international position, Stalin began to switch the emphasis of his foreign policy towards some form of accommodation with those capitalist powers which also felt threatened by a reviving Germany in Europe and Japanese aggression in the Far East. The Soviet Union's exclusion from the ultimately abortive negotiations for a Four Power Pact in 1933 and Hitler's conclusion of a non-aggression pact with Poland in 1934 made this more urgent. The first obvious sign of this change in approach was the softening of tone towards the League of Nations which the USSR joined on September 18, 1934. From this point on, the policy of 'collective security' was vociferously followed by the Soviet authorities in general and Litvinov in particular.

Phase 5: 1934 to August 1939

What must be made clear at this point is that although political relations with Nazi Germany were very poor, the economic links between the two nations continued. For example another important trade agreement was signed on 20 March 1934. Furthermore, we know from the captured German documents that in 1935, 1936, 1937 and 1939 when Soviet and German officials held their routine economic meetings, the Soviet side suggested that it might be opportune to improve political relations. These suggestions were turned down by the Germans, but it is quite clear that Stalin was prepared to court the Nazis in secret, whilst espousing collective security in public. A final decision on which way to jump could be left until later, while the Soviet Union's ability to defend itself continued to grow.

Stalin moved further towards the West in 1935 when the USSR signed the mutual assistant pacts with France and Czechoslovakia. Given the political geography of Eastern Europe, quite how the USSR was actually supposed to bring its weight to bear on Germany in an international crisis was something of a mystery: the illusion of having a counterweight seemed enough for the French, and for the Soviet Union to be included in such a security system was progress indeed. The agreements included a clause which made it clear that the USSR was only to act if requested to do so by the French. In line with this diplomatic realignment, the Comintern also switched its tactics, now instructing its puppet communist parties to support the policy of the Popular Front, namely cooperation with any political party which was anti-fascist.

However, from 1934 to 1939 Stalin drew little benefit from his new policy. Time after time, the British and French chose not to stand firm in the face of aggressive moves by Italy, Japan or Germany, the three powers who had by 1937 created the Anti-Comintern Pact, which was clearly aimed at the USSR. This is not the place to analyse the policy of appeasement, but it is not hard to imagine the conclusions being drawn in Moscow as Italy took

Ethiopia, Japan seized more of China in 1937, and Hitler remilitarised the Rhineland in 1936, absorbing Austria in early 1938. Was this a deliberate attempt by Britain and France to push the aggressive states towards Russia, as the Soviet press constantly claimed? Was Stalin in a position to assume anything else, as after all, four Soviet suggestions for an international conference between March and September 1938 had simply been ignored by Britain and France? The Munich agreement of October 1938 must have been almost the last straw for Stalin, as throughout the summer crisis he had been assuring the French of Soviet support; yet the French ignored its ally the USSR and followed the British lead in handing over the Sudetenland to Hitler. The Soviet Union was once again excluded from European decision-making, despite being in the League, and despite having concluded mutual assistance pacts with France and Czechoslovakia.

The USSR had no common border with Czechoslovakia and Stalin had recently purged the officer corps of the Red Army, making effective Soviet intervention somewhat improbable; but this did not alter the fact that unlike Britain and France, the USSR could publicly present itself as the only power prepared to stand firm against Nazi aggression. Whether this was a bluff or not, all we know is that the bluff was never called.

The USSR had also managed to reap considerable propaganda rewards from the Spanish civil war. Why did Stalin involve the USSR in this war which was so far away from Soviet borders? There are several possibilities. He may have wished to:

- create a Soviet satellite in Spain;
- preserve the democratically elected Republican government;
- demonstrate his belief in collective security by helping to thwart fascist aggression; or
- show that the USSR was now an international force to be reckoned with.

The first two seem to be the most improbable, but some combination of the others may provide an acceptable explanation. Though the USSR signed the non-intervention agreement, large amounts of military aid were sent to the Republic, but never enough to guarantee a Republican victory. Perhaps Stalin was showing his customary caution by testing the resolve of Britain and France who, as it happened, were prepared to stand aside and let the Republic take its chances without them. Apart from propaganda value, what did Stalin get out of the Spanish episode? One unexpected bonus was the Spanish government's gold reserves. More importantly, the three years of war gave him additional insights into the attitudes of his ally, France, and his collective security partner, Great Britain. From a Soviet point of view it became obvious that these two powers would accept quite severe risks to their respective strategic positions rather than take effective action against Italy or Germany. Unfortunately for the USSR and unlike Hitler, Stalin could not fully benefit from the military experience gained in the war, because he murdered a number of those officers who had served in Spain, and tended to ignore the lessons that the Germans learned so well.

Thus, by the time of Hitler's seizure of the rump of Czechoslovakia in March 1939, apart from a certain propaganda success, Stalin had absolutely nothing to show for his policy of collective security. Worse still, no accommodation had yet proved possible with Nazi Germany, which was now immeasurably stronger than it had been in 1933. As if to emphasise the USSR's dangerous position, 1938 and 1939 had seen Japan launch very substantial attacks on the Soviet Far East. The USSR had won the battle around Lake Khasan in 1938 and Khalkin-Gol in 1939 which led the Japanese to think twice about any further adventure in the area, but despite a neutrality treaty with Japan in April 1941, Stalin could not be sure of his Far Eastern frontier until late 1941, when his brilliant agent in Tokyo, Richard Sorge, told him that the Japanese had other plans.

And yet from being isolated and ignored in 1938 and early 1939, Stalin suddenly found himself in the extraordinary position of being courted by both of Europe's power blocs. The last moments of the collective security policy came between March and August of 1939. This began with another failed Soviet suggestion for an international conference, continued as an Anglo-French military delegation unsuccessfully tried to negotiate its way towards a joint agreement with the USSR and ended with the 'bombshell' of the Nazi-Soviet pact on 23 August.

Why did Stalin decide to become an ally of Hitler and not of Britain and France? A key factor must have been the utter lack of resolution shown by these two powers over the previous six years. Was it in any way credible that either of them would stand by their guarantee of Poland in the face of increasing German pressure? Neither Hitler nor Stalin thought so. It was to Stalin's great, but temporary, good fortune that his attempts to improve Soviet-German relations suddenly bore fruit. Hitler was anxious to thwart any Anglo-French moves to involve the USSR in a military pact and he was planning to attack Poland on 1 September. Ribbentrop made Stalin an offer that was impossible to refuse. The Soviet-German commercial treaty of 18 August was swiftly followed by the non-aggression pact of 23 August. The secret sections of this pact, in essence, gave the USSR eastern Poland, the three Baltic states and Bessarabia. The treaty also put off the likelihood of a war with

Germany for some time. All that Britain and France could have offered was the strong possibility of a war with Germany in the very near future and presumably on the same side as the old enemy Poland. Stalin had learned the value of mutual assistance pacts with the French in 1938. What other decision could he have made in the circumstances?

Phase 6: 23 August 1939 to 22 June 1941

In the course of the next 20 months Hitler extended his control over most of Europe by military might, economic penetration and alliance. By the early summer of 1941 he was ready to launch his long dreamed-of attack on his temporary ally, the USSR. How had Stalin used his time? Vast deliveries of grain, petroleum and other vital strategic materials had been sent to Germany as part of the trade agreements between the two governments, but the Germans had only sporadically kept to their side of the bargain. On 17 September the Red Army occupied its allotted zone of Poland. Between November 1939 and March 1940 Finland was battered into ceding territory to the USSR and by the end of 1940, Estonia, Latvia and Lithuania had been absorbed. The USSR had gained much, but it had lost the moral superiority it had spuriously claimed ever since 1917, and had now demonstrated the Soviet imperialism which was so marked in Eastern Europe after 1945. More disturbingly for Stalin, the Red Army had performed abysmally in the war against Finland, and a rapid programme of reorganisation had been put into action. That Stalin expected and feared a war with Germany is clear, but during this period he did as much as he could to appease Hitler. It is true that there was some tough jockeying for position in the Balkans between Stalin and Hitler, but the USSR agreed to join the Tripartite Pact which linked her with Japan, Italy and Germany in a vague but grandiose scheme which promised Stalin gains in Central Asia. The deliveries of strategic materials to Germany continued until a few hours before the German attack on the USSR. It seemed as though Stalin was desperate to avoid giving the Germans an excuse to attack, even though there can be no doubt that Stalin was in receipt of some very high grade intelligence material on German plans. It is still a mystery why Stalin, who trusted no one and had murdered millions, could not accept that Hitler would attack him when he did. Perhaps even dictators are prone to wishful thinking, and certainly there was nobody in Stalin's court who would risk his career and life by contradicting him. On 22 June 1941, after 20 years of constantly expressed fear of foreign intervention, 'the world's first workers' state' was again attacked by a coalition of imperialist powers, this time led by Nazi Germany.

The catastrophe which Operation Barbarossa began, came within a few weeks and a few miles of destroying the Soviet Union and probably Stalin himself, but this is not the place to catalogue the dreadful suffering of the Soviet population during the Great Patriotic War, nor to deal with the emergence of the USSR as a superpower after 1945.

Conclusion

How can we assess the success or failure of Soviet foreign policy between the wars? If the overriding aim of the Soviet leadership had been to avoid being attacked, then it had failed disastrously by June 1941. But to a large extent much of the manoeuvring of the Narkomindel throughout the entire interwar period had been from a position of weakness. The USSR was rarely able to influence world events and indeed was often simply ignored at key moments, while being seen as useful at other times. It is true that the Soviet Union derived real benefit from its economic relationship with Germany throughout the period and that the secret military links had been valuable. The non-aggression pact with Hitler had also given Stalin a chance to expand his borders, but it was invariably Germany who called the tune. Perhaps this alliance had given Stalin a breathing space, but one is entitled to ask whether the time gained was used fully. Paradoxically, it was Stalin who must take the responsibility both for the disaster which almost overwhelmed the USSR in 1941 and for ultimate victory which could not have been won without the industrial base created in the 1930s. For Stalin the lesson was clear. The Soviet Union had to be economically and militarily strong before she could either survive or play any significant role in world affairs.

Patrick Condren is Head of History at Eltham College.

John Whittam
The Origins of the
Second World War

A number of different, if linked, conflicts in different theatres have traditionally been ascribed the general title of the Second World War. John Whittam explores the deep roots of these conflicts and makes the case for arguing that the Second World War only really began when it became a global war in 1941.

On 27 September 1940, Japan, Italy and Germany signed the Tripartite Pact in Tokyo. This may seem a perverse way to begin a discussion of the origins of the Second World War; it may also be seen as eloquent proof that since 1989 historians appear to have contracted a kind of anniversary mania. There is nothing new in this. Indeed, some years ago a group of historians published a book on the origins of the war to commemorate the publication of a book on the origins of the war! They were celebrating the 25th anniversary of A. J. P. Taylor's controversial refutation of the theory that the war which began in September 1939 can be explained quite simply by calling it 'Hitler's War'. Deliberately provocative – and we must include his often-quoted remark that Hitler stumbled into war 'through launching on 29 August a diplomatic manoeuvre which he ought to have launched on 28 August' – he forced a re-examination of the impact of the First World War, of the diplomacy of the inter-war period, of the phenomenon of appeasement and of the short- and long-term objectives of German foreign policy and military planning. Taylor's 1961 book certainly stimulated further research. His critics were quick to point out that he had paid insufficient attention to economic factors or to ideology and some objected to his manipulation of the documentary evidence. They then proceeded to write their own interpretations. It was a controversy which yielded rich dividends, and not just in royalties for the authors.

European origins

But in one sense Taylor and his critics did their readers a disservice. Their apparent preoccupation with European issues left them open to the charge of parochialism, if indeed they claimed to be examining the origins of a *world* war. Like Taylor's own book many of these studies stopped short in September 1939. All this tended to confirm the commonly-held view in the west that the European war which began with the invasion of Poland on 1 September was synonymous with the world war which ended in 1945. But the wars which were fought between September 1939 and June 1940 took place in Poland, Scandinavia, the Low Countries and France. With Mussolini's entry into the war on 10 June 1940 the Mediterranean became a war theatre which involved North Africa, the Balkans and the Middle East. If Britain survived, the area of possible conflict had considerably widened. But as the Tripartite Pact was being signed in September 1940 the actual combatants, apart from Britain's Commonwealth allies, remained European, Britain herself, Germany and Italy. Over the next few months Greece and Yugoslavia must be added to this list, but both had been crushed by the Axis powers by the spring of the following year. Japan and the Soviet Union, both aligned with Berlin and Rome, remained aloof and so did the United States, despite whatever 'Special Relationship' she may have had with Britain. Only the participation of at least two of them would produce a global war.

Globalisation of war

The next phase of the European war began with Hitler's invasion of Russia, the implementation of Operation Barbarossa on 22 June 1941. If Japan had decided to strike north at the Soviet Union this would have produced a conflict which would not be inaccurately described as a world war, but Japan had signed a non-aggression pact with Moscow the previous April and, after some hesitation, decided to adhere to it. In July 1941 the Japanese had occupied southern Indo-China (they had garrisoned the north a year earlier after the fall of France, a clear indication of the links which existed between events in Europe and Asia) and this prompted Washington to impose a *de facto* oil embargo on Japan and to freeze all her assets. To survive as a great independent power Japan made plans to strike south to secure the oil and other resources of the Dutch East Indies, Malaya and the Philippines. This set Japan on a collision course with the United States as well as with Britain and on 22 August Tokyo drew up a strategy for the neutralisation of the American Pacific fleet at Pearl Harbor. As the Japanese moved into southern Indo-China, American forces occupied Iceland. This was part of an escalating undeclared war against German U-boats in the Atlantic which were intercepting American supplies destined for Britain under the terms of the Lend Lease Act of March 1941. So when Roosevelt met Churchill off Newfoundland in August 1941 to draw up the Atlantic Charter, there was a very real possibility that America might find herself at war either in the Atlantic or the Pacific or both. But isolationist sentiment was still strong in the United States and Hitler ordered his naval commanders to show restraint. It was left to the Japanese, increasingly anxious about their oil reserves, to make the fateful decision to attack Pearl Harbor on 7 December 1941 and to invade American, Dutch and British possessions in south-east Asia. On 11 December Japan's partners in the Tripartite Pact, Germany and Italy, declared war on the United States. The Second World War had begun. Understandably, Russia was not eager to enter the war in Asia until Germany was crushed. This was accomplished in May 1945 and in August, in the interval between the dropping of atomic bombs on Hiroshima and Nagasaki, Russia declared war on Japan just days before surrender.

By September 1945, when the formal Japanese surrender took place, another war – soon to be called the Cold War – had begun, an old war in China – already decades old – had been resumed, and new wars in Vietnam and Korea were about to start. With its VE and VJ Days, 1945 soon seemed less of a watershed between war and peace than many people had hoped. But despite these uncertainties historians have to be content with it and recognise 1945 as a significant landmark denoting the conclusion of a series of wars which by December 1941 could be given the generic title of Second World War.

The deep roots of war

A meticulous inquiry into the origins of the European war of 1939–41 and the world war of 1941–45 would require the investigation of no less than eight distinct wars in the earlier period and four for the later. They all have direct or indirect links with one another but each one also has specific causes. To give two examples: the British and French declarations of war on Germany in September 1939, the Russian invasion of Finland two months later and Mussolini's attack on Greece in October 1940 cannot easily be fitted into a single bland generalisation and each demands at least some individual treatment and specialist knowledge; the same is true in investigating the reasons for the Japanese attack on the United States and Britain on 7 December 1941 and the German declaration of war on America four days later. These are difficult problems but it is possible to solve some of them. In the excellent Longman series on the origins of modern wars, Philip Bell has written on *The Origins of the Second World War in Europe* and Akira Iriye on *The Origins of the Second World War in Asia and the Pacific*. Bell concentrates on the period 1932–41 and Iriye from 1921–41. They are both very sound and readable accounts but the danger is that the one with the swastika on the cover will be more widely read than the one with a damaged warship at Pearl Harbor. This will preserve the imbalance that was noted in the debate between Taylor and his critics. One author has attempted to combine Europe, America and Asia by focusing on Germany, the United States and Japan: William Carr's *Poland to Pearl Harbor: The Making of the Second World War* is also interesting because one of his main themes is the evolution of the Second World War out of the European and other wars which preceded it. Indeed, his title suggests that the Second World War of 1941 was caused by the European war which began with the invasion of Poland. That it was a major cause is indisputable and this makes it even more essential to understand the origins of the conflict which broke out after September 1939.

Most of the problems of the twentieth century were created by the collapse of five empires between 1911 and 1923. The first to disintegrate was the crumbling Manchu empire which left China as a gigantic power vacuum which the Japanese sought to fill if European and American rivals would allow it. The other four collapsed during the First World War. The fall of the Second Reich, the Habsburg Monarchy and Tsarist Russia – all defeated in war – left central and eastern Europe as a dangerous power vacuum which a revived Germany sought to fill with momentous consequences in the late 1930s. The destruction of the Ottoman Empire helped to destabilise the Middle East, which was rapidly becoming a centre of world attention because of its strategic position and its vast reserves of oil. The First World War also witnessed two crucially important events. In the spring of 1917 the United States entered the war and for the next three years played an active role as a world power. The experience of this war and disillusionment with the peace which followed it determined most Americans not to repeat the experiment. American abstention from political and military involvement in European affairs between 1920 and 1942 is an important negative factor in explaining the coming of war in 1939. In the autumn of 1917, the Bolshevik revolution led to the formation of the Soviet Union with its professed aim of stimulating world revolution, an aim which could be furthered by the Marxist belief in the inevitability of war among capitalist states. The aggressive rhetoric of this new ideological state and the Communist parties which sprang up throughout the world, not only created universal fear and instability but tended to mask the Kremlin's basic *Realpolitik* and the essentially defensive posture necessary for the political and economic survival of the Soviet Union.

Consequences of the First World War

There are still more consequences of the First World War to consider. Because of the horrors of the Western Front, the death and mutilation of millions of soldiers and civilians from Belgium to the Ukraine, and the destruction and disruption of economic life, the agonised cry of 'Never Again' was heard everywhere. That this must be the war to end all wars was a universal hope. The terrible efficiency of the killing machines, the improved firepower of artillery and machine guns, the use of poison gas, the invention of the tank and the terrifying appearance of warplanes dropping bombs, led to urgent calls for disarmament. Civilisation itself was at stake. Unfortunately, the faith placed in the new League of Nations, and the disarmament conferences in Washington 1921–22 and Geneva 1932–34, served only to encourage the warlike instincts of those who were dissatified and disgusted with the peace settlement of 1919. In similar fashion the policy of appeasement in the late 1930s acted as a stimulus to those who sought to redress their grievances, real or imagined, by brutal blackmail or military force.

Even in 1919 there were pessimists. Marshal Foch described the Peace of Versailles as merely a twenty-years truce. If this is true – and it appears a remarkably accurate prophecy – the conflict after 1939 was simply the continuation of the First World War. This has inspired some historians to develop the concept of another Thirty Years' War 1914–45 but, unlike the events of 1618–48, with Germany as an active rather than a passive agent. In the case of eastern Asia it is possible to think in terms of a Fifty Years' War, beginning with Japan's defeat of China in 1895 and ending with Japan's defeat in 1945. But in both cases a significant interlude, the period 1922–31 for the Sino-Japanese conflict and from 1919 to the late 1930s in the case of Germany and its European neighbours, does occur. The problem with a theory of continuity is that it makes the renewal of war appear inevitable. In fact, in the 1920s both Tokyo and Berlin showed a willingness to collaborate with other powers in seeking peaceful and negotiated settlements to their difficulties. The erosion of this willingness, through internal and external developments, explains the recourse to war. Although the area for manoeuvre shrank during the 1930s, opportunities for the avoidance of the fateful decisions of 1939 and 1941 continued to exist.

Failings of Versailles

President Wilson's aim to make the world safe for democracy was not realised. Lenin and the Comintern proposed a rival ideology, and in eastern Europe and most of the Third World, authoritarian methods became or remained prevalent. In 1922 Mussolini became Prime Minister in Italy and Fascism emerged to challenge both bourgeois democracy and Communism. Its strident nationalism, its glorification of war and violence and its dependence on the whims of the Duce made it a disturbing factor in international relations and its admirers in other countries contributed to the polarisation of domestic politics. In the early 1930s Japanese militarists and civilian nationalists asserted their dominance over more moderate, democratic forces. In 1933 Hitler became Chancellor of the Third Reich and his racist ideology, combined with the growing economic and military strength of the country, made Nazi Germany an even greater threat to peace and stability than the Soviet Union, Italy and Japan. Ideology cannot be ignored in any consideration of the origins of the war, even if *Realpolitik* often seemed to override it. Hitler's racial war against the Jews and the Slavs and other inferior races took precedence over everything else in the later phases of the war. Scarce railway stock was used to transport Jews to extermination camps instead of troops or weapons to the war fronts. But ill-digested Darwinian or other pseudo-scientific theories concerning the survival of the fittest were not the monopoly of Hitler, Himmler and the SS, nor were nationalistic beliefs in a natural hierarchy of superior and inferior nations and peoples confined to the Fascist or authoritarian states. Britian only gave up southern Ireland with great reluctance and after much blood-shed, and Churchill in the 1930s was determined to prevent India achieving self-rule. Some nations were obviously born to rule, a view shared by the French and most other Europeans, South Africans, North and South Americans – always provided they were white. It was a view which had infuriated the Japanese at the Paris and Washington conferences when they were regarded as part of the 'yellow peril' but one which they shared when they in turn contemplated the Chinese and the Koreans and – a little later – the cowardly Europeans of Tientsin, Shanghai, Hong Kong and Singapore.

President Wilson had included national self-determination as part of the democratic process. In Eastern Europe new nation states appeared but drawing ethnic boundaries proved to be difficult and contentious. In 1919 the defeated Reich saw millions of Germans forced to live under alien rule in Poland, Czechoslovakia, Italy and elsewhere. Even within the borders of the new Weimar Germany, Berlin did not exercise full sovereignty over the demilitarised zone in the Rhineland. Significantly, after establishing his political control and rearming Germany in 1935 in defiance of Versailles, Hitler marched into the Rhineland in 1936, annexed independent Austria, again in defiance of Versailles in March 1938, and then proceeded to break up the Czech and Polish states. After all, he was only implementing President Wilson's doctrine of self-determination. So many other national groups longed to emulate the Germans that Eastern Europe seethed with discontent so that even the genius of

Lord Runciman and the appeasement policies of Chamberlain and Daladier proved inadequate. As in 1914, ethnic rivalries produced a local war which swiftly escalated into a European war, and as over the Serbian crisis of June/July 1914 so over the Polish crisis of March to September 1939: the diplomats came under close scrutiny for allowing this to happen.

Descent into war

President Wilson had called for open covenants openly arrived at as part of his attempt to inaugurate a new era in international relations. This was as unsuccessful as his appeals for democracy and national self-determination. American refusal to accept the Versailles settlement was a severe blow but for more than a decade the Washington and London naval conferences, the operation of the League of Nations, the signing of the Treaty of Locarno in 1925, the Kellogg-Briand Peace Pact of 1928 and the disarmament conference which met in Geneva in 1932, seemed to offer the promise of a New Diplomacy which would help to outlaw war. But in the same period there was abundant evidence that the old diplomacy which many regarded as the basic cause of the war of 1914 and the failure of the peace of 1919 was still in operation. The Russo-German treaties of Rapallo in 1922 and of Berlin in 1926 and the clandestine military cooperation between them, the treaties signed by France and Poland, Czechoslovakia and Yugoslavia and the Little Entente grouping in central Europe all seemed alarmingly familiar. Things grew worse in the 1930s. The League and other forms of negotiation failed to check Japanese aggression in Manchura after 1931; in 1933 both Germany and Japan left the League; in 1934 the Disarmament conference ended after two years of fruitless argument; in 1935 Mussolini invaded Ethiopia and League sanctions proved abortive; in the same year Germany reintroduced conscription and, with the failure of the other Locarno signatories at Stresa, Britain signed a naval agreement with Germany in June. In 1936 Hitler sent troops into the Rhineland and the Spanish Civil War broke out. The war in Spain which neither the League nor the Non-Intervention Committee could stop soon involved Germany, Italy and Russia and – indirectly – the French and British. For many it was an ideological war between fascism and anti-fascism, for others it was the start of yet another European war with the great powers manoeuvring for advantage. It ended with a victory for the Nationalist forces of Franco in March 1939 just six months before the Polish war but, like the war in Ethiopia, it is a crucial event in the history of the interwar period if only because it converted so many pacifists and other antiwar groups and parties of the left and centre to the view that in a just war they had an obligation to fight. 'Arms for Spain' became the cry of those who had condemned the 'merchants of death', the arms manufacturers, for their promotion of war. Meanwhile, a much bigger war had broken out in Asia. This was the grotesquely named 'China Incident' in 1937,the Japanese war for the control of mainland China which lasted until 1945.

The Russian enigma

By 1939 the diplomacy of peace through the League, through negotiated settlements, through appeasement political or economic – had signally failed. Japan, Germany and Italy, who all regarded themselves as 'have-not' powers pitted against the plutocratic empires of Britain, France and America, drew closer together and made their own diplomatic arrangements. In the autumn of 1936, Mussolini proclaimed the existence of a Rome-Berlin Axis and Germany and Japan signed the Anti-Comintern Pact directed against Russia. Italy joined this a year later. The leaders of these three master races were confident that they had the strength and the will to overpower their three democratic rivals, symbolised by Roosevelt in his wheelchair, Chamberlain clutching an umbrella and Daladier with a glass in his hand. Stalin was an enigma. In the summer of 1938 and again in 1939, Japanese troops fought a border war against Russia to the west, and then to the east of their puppet state of Manchukuo, and lost. Despite the massive purge of the Red Army by Stalin, the Russian forces so impressed Tokyo that plans for further attacks in the north were indefinitely postponed. In the event, they never took place. The Japanese moved south and launched the global war already discussed and the Russian troops moved west to bring the Wehrmacht to a halt in front of Leningrad and Moscow. These obscure border wars with casualties of perhaps 20,000 are as important as the Ethiopian and Spanish wars and cannot be ignored in assessing the diplomacy of the period or the origins of the wars in Europe and Asia.

Britain and France were also perplexed by Stalin's Russia. After Hitler's destruction of the rump Czech state in March 1939 Chamberlain began to realise that the German leader was perhaps intent upon more than just the revision of Versailles. Hitler might, Chamberlain said in a speech in Birmingham, be thinking of world domination. To draw the line, Chamberlain guaranteed the independence of Poland at the end of March 1939; reluctantly, he agreed to explore the possibility of an alignment with Russia to give more credibility to the guarantee. Anglo-French talks in Moscow during the summer, while Hitler relentlessly pursued the Polish issue, came to nothing. Russo-German trade talks which had been proceeding simultaneously – in secret – now took on supreme importance, as Hitler had set himself a deadline for attacking Poland at the end of August. Hitler seized upon Stalin's suggestion of a political agreement and urged the Soviet leader to receive foreign minister Ribbentrop before 23 August. This was accepted and on that day the Nazi-Soviet Pact was signed. A secret protocol arranged for the partition of Poland and the Baltic states. The pact was intended to deter Britain and France from honouring their guarantees to Poland, but in this it failed. Tokyo and Rome were as shocked by the pact as London and Paris. Hitler had been trying to convert the Anti-Comintern Pact into a Tripartite Pact, but the Japanese had been unwilling to antagonise the western powers when war with Russia seemed imminent. After Italy's surprise invasion of Albania, Germany and Italy had signed the Pact of Steel in May 1939. Japan still refused to join and the news of the German-Russian agreement led to the collapse of the pro-German government, a ceasefire with Russia on 16 September (and it was no coincidence that Stalin invaded eastern Poland on 17 September – but yet another example of the interaction of events in Mongolia, Tokyo, Moscow and Berlin) and conciliatory moves towards the western democracies. German victories in Poland and western Europe forced the Italians and Japanese to hide their resentment at Hitler's cavalier behaviour and in September 1940 they signed the Tripartite Pact.

Economic origins of war

President Wilson's attempt to construct a new order based on democracy, national self-determination and open diplomacy was unlikely to succeed – so he and all other presidents and secretaries of state tended to believe – unless the American policy of the Open Door was universally accepted. This economic doctrine called for free access to markets and raw materials. It deplored the existence of closed economic systems, currency blocs, exchange controls and anything that prevented the free flow of money and goods. It had first been explicitly enunciated when American traders peered excitedly at the mirage of the vast Chinese market at the turn of the century. It had become one of Wilson's Fourteen Points and one of Roosevelt's aims in the Atlantic Charter. For Cordell Hull, Secretary of State 1932–44, the business of the State Department was business.

The economic crisis and high inflation of the early 1920s, which had helped Mussolini into power and almost destroyed the Weimar Republic, prompted the Americans to intervene in Europe with schemes such as the Dawes Plan in 1924 and the Young Plan in 1929. American isolationism never prevented economic involvement with Europe and the rest of the world. The attempt to stabilise the economic and political situation came to an abrupt end, however, with the crash on Wall Street in October 1929. The Open Door was slammed shut as each country tried to survive the Great Depression by measures of self-sufficiency, protective tariffs, imperial preference – as in the Ottawa agreements of 1932 in relation to the Dominions and Empire – and currency controls. World trade shrank and millions became unemployed. This helped Hitler into power with his schemes for a New Order, first in Germany and then in the rest of Europe and perhaps beyond. It helped the Japanese militarists to push forward with plans for an East Asian Co-Prosperity Sphere. It confirmed the wisdom of Stalin's Socialism in One Country and Mussolini's drive for autarchy. In the United States it led to the New Deal and in Britain to the National government and the abandonment of free trade and the Gold Standard. None of this made war inevitable but the consequences of the Depression certainly made the maintenance of peace more difficult.

The three self-styled 'have-not nations' possessed governments prepared to fight their way out of the economic crisis. Aggressiveness and expansionism were already integral ingredients in their ideologies; economic survival at the expense of weaker neighbours and the effete empires of the democracies was equally compelling. Germany and Japan made rearmament their top priority and devised offensive military plans. Britain, France and the US sought to avoid an arms race which would further destabilise their economies and they adopted defensive military strategies. The Maginot Line was less of a threat to peace than the panzer divisions of the Third Reich. In Ethiopia, Spain and China the tripartite powers revealed their willingness to bomb civilian targets as well as military. Fear that 'the bomber will always get through' helps to explain the reluctance of the democracies to go to war. During 1931–41 they responded to the initiative of the aggressor powers, hoping at first to restore the transient equilibrium of the 1920s and, when this failed, to defend themselves. The British and French declarations of war against Germany were defensive; the Phoney War which followed proves this. Blockade, bombing – or the threat of it – and the overheating of the German economy would, it was believed, result in the overthrow of Hitler by the Germans themselves.

Conclusion

This was a gross miscalculation. France fell but Britain fought on. Even Russian moves into Poland and, although it sounds a contradiction in terms, Russia's war against Finland, were essentially defensive. Japan, however, deliberately launched wars in Manchuria and China in 1931 and 1937, and at Pearl Harbor and in south-east Asia in December 1941. Italy waged wars of aggression against Ethiopia and Albania in 1935 and 1939, against Britain, France and Greece in 1940, and against Russia and the US in 1941. Nazi Germany attacked Poland in 1939, Denmark, Norway, The Netherlands, Luxemburg, Belgium, France and Britain in 1940, and Yugoslavia, Greece, Russia and the US in 1941. The judges on the war crimes tribunals at Nuremberg and Tokyo after the war were not called upon to make agonisingly difficult decisions about where the guilt really lay.

However, when the three aggressor powers signed their Tripartite Pact in September 1940 there were then only two local wars being fought, an Anglo-German war in the west which was about to spread to include an Anglo-Italian war in the Mediterranean, and a Sino-Japanese war in the Far East. Hitler was planning to invade the Soviet Union but had not finalised it – that was in December 1940 – Japan was contemplating a non-aggression pact with Russia – implemented in April 1941 – and a war against the democracies but no final decision was to be made until the summer and autumn of 1941. Mussolini was in the process of fighting his 'parallel war' but not even he knew what this implied. It was not absolutely certain that the existing wars would escalate into a global war. It was the decisions the aggressor powers subsequently took that led to the start of the Second World War in 1941.

Further Reading

Bell, P. M. H. *The Origins of the Second World War in Europe* (Longman, 1986).

Boyce, R. and Robertson, E. M. (eds) *Paths to War* (Macmillan, 1989).

Carr, W. *Poland to Pearl Harbor* (Arnold, 1985).

Iriye, A. *The Origins of the Second World War in Asia and the Pacific* (Longman, 1987).

Martel, G. (ed.) *The Origins of the Second World War Reconsidered* (Allen and Unwin, 1986).

Taylor, A. J. P. *The Origins of the Second World War* (Hamish Hamilton, 1961).

Watt, D. C. *How War Came* (Heinemann, 1989).

John Whittam teaches History at the University of Bristol.

Jessica Saraga
Examiner's Report

An analysis of this essay on Stalin illustrates it is important not only to assess the achievements of historical figures, but also to analyse them in the context of their aims and legacies.

Question

By what methods and to what extent did Stalin effect economic and social change in the Soviet Union during the 1930s?

Student's answer by 'Ayesha'

The 1930s was a time of great change in the Soviet Union. It saw the transformation of vast land in a post-revolutionary duality to a country that became the second most powerful industrial nation in the world. Such a remarkable feat was achieved within the incredible timespan of ten years. It defies all description and comprehension. However it was only through heroic self-sacrifice, dedicated patriotism, and ruthless discipline, cruel, sadistic and corrupt party and police officials, that such feats were achieved. The cost was enormous, and was to leave a scar on Soviet society that is yet to really heal today, fifty years on.

In principle, this is a promising beginning. Ayesha takes an overview of the 1930s, which is the period covered in the essay question, and makes some general points in answer to the question, which she will, presumably, follow up in detail later. She addresses the question by hinting at both the methods ('ruthless discipline') and the extent ('transformation') called for by the question.

It's a pity that she doesn't match the confidence of her approach with an equally confident way of expressing herself. What may have struck you most, in fact, was her confusing terminology, particularly in her second sentence. Surely she means 'vast amounts of land'? And what is a 'post-revolutionary duality'? I imagine Ayesha means that the USSR developed industry as well as agriculture; it would have been clearer if she'd said just that!

I should also have liked to have seen a distinction in the list of what was necessary for all this to be achieved, between the positive factors ('heroic self-sacrifice', 'dedicated patriotism') and the negative ones ('ruthless discipline . . . etc'). Ayesha should make it clear that the self-sacrifice and patriotism came from ordinary Russian people, but the discipline and corruption was imposed upon them.

Ayesha goes a bit over the top with her 'incredible' timespan (It can't be incredible if it happened!) and her 'It defies all description and comprehension'. If it really can't be described and understood, then she might as well give up her essay now! You should try to resist this kind of hyperbole (exaggeration for effect), which is easy to fall into, but which distorts your meaning. Ayesha could have omitted the word 'incredible' and left the sentence just as effective, since it still includes the word 'remarkable', which is much more appropriate.

Stalin told the central committee in November 1928 'to achieve the final victory of socialism in our country we need to catch up and overhaul those countries in the technical, economic and industrial sense. Either we do it, or we shall be crushed.' Communists had consistently defined a 'socialist' society as a highly industrialised society, in which the means of production were nationalised and planned. Stalin continued to shrewdly use and over-play a threat to Soviet power to create an atmosphere of nervous tension, which along with terror and ruthless discipline could now be funnelled into achieving economic goals previously seen as impossible. In a later speech in early 1931 Stalin repeated, 'One feature of the history of old Russia was the continual beating she suffered because of her backwardness . . . We are fifty or a hundred years behind the advanced countries. We must catch up this distance in ten years. Either we do it or we go under.'

Ayesha now begins her essay proper by setting the scene just before the 1930s began. 1928 is a good starting point because it was in this year that Stalin finally established himself in supreme power in the USSR. He had successfully fought off the political rivalry of Kamenev, Zinoviev and Trotsky, and gained the support of a majority of the Politburo.

The first Five Year Plan was instigated in December 1928, when national economic goals were set spanning most fields of economic life. In the end the five year plan lasted for four years, beginning in October 1928 and ending in December 1932. The peasantry perhaps experienced the greatest and most radical Stalinist reforms. A system of collectivisation was introduced in 1928 to create larger and more productive mechanised farms involving reducing very sharply the number of collection points and bringing them under much stricter control. Richer peasants, the Kulaks, were eliminated as a class under the new system of collectivisation. The Kulaks were trapped in a catch-22 situation.

Having to give up their land, they were not allowed to join the collective farm movements. They were labelled as 'the sworn enemies of socialism'. In dealing with the Kulaks, Stalin's ruthless determination in establishing the Soviet Union as a world economic power regardless of the cost of human life or welfare is clearly evident. Five million Kulaks and their families were deported to inhospitable regions of the Soviet Union where many died of starvation or were killed. Stalin was sadistically frank and brutally open when it came to the Kulaks, 'it is ridiculous and foolish to talk at length about dekulakisation . . . When the head is off one does not grieve for the hair.'

The next section of Ayesha's essay deals with the first Five Year Plan. In fact, having said that the plan spanned most fields of economic life, she then concentrates on only one aspect of it: collectivisation. She describes events well, and explains them in terms of Stalin's 'ruthless determination' to establish the Soviet Union as a world power regardless of human cost, with another illuminating quotation from Stalin himself. However, she doesn't go very deeply into the reasons for Stalin's decision to liquidate the Kulaks. Could they not have been allowed to join the collectives in preference to deportation and death? In fact Stalin was already showing the inability to tolerate opposition which was to become a pathological paranoia later in the 1930s. Eventually no one could disagree with him and survive. Ayesha only hints at this, in her reference to Stalin's being 'sadistically frank and brutally open'. You may have noticed this piece of classic – but unnecessary – tautology (saying exactly the same thing more than once in different ways).

Having effectively put himself in charge, Stalin could set about improving the economy, which, as Ayesha explains with her quotations, he saw as vital to the successful establishment of socialism. One of his disagreements with Trotsky had been on the question of whether it was possible to create 'socialism in one country', a country surrounded by capitalist countries. Trotsky believed it was not possible, and had insisted on the need to export the revolution to the other countries in Europe in order for socialism to survive. Eventually he thought, with optimistic idealism, socialism would spread to the rest of the world. Stalin was now setting out to prove that socialism in one country was attainable, and that Trotsky was wrong. Ayesha uses quotations from Stalin to explain that he believed that the only way for a socialist country to survive in a capitalist world was to become economically as powerful as the capitalists. In an examination essay she would not have access to these quotations to make her points, and would have to explain Stalin's thinking in her own words.

She slips in an interesting point here, that 'communists had consistently defined a socialist society as a highly industrialised society'. She is quite right; this idea of socialism goes back to Marx himself, who believed that socialism could only be achieved in an advanced industrial country.

Industrial workers could take control of the means of production more easily than agricultural workers, whose organisation and class consciousness were not so well developed, largely because of the difficulties in communication involved in being scattered over large areas of countryside rather than concentrated in towns.

Another stylistic point is Ayesha's cliché 'catch-22 situation'. A cliché is a phrase so well used that it loses its meaning. Although Ayesha has in fact used the phrase in its original sense (from the Joseph Heller novel about the Second World War) of a situation in which whatever you do, there is no way out, the concept transfers uneasily to the grimness of Stalin's Russia.

More seriously, Ayesha has not followed up her discussion of collectivisation and 'de-kulakisation' by saying what were its effects economically. She should explain that the passive resistance of the peasants by refusing to sow grain and slaughtering their animals led to widespread famine in 1931–2. In agriculture, the first five year plan was not a success. The sentiment in the first sentence of Ayesha's next paragraph is therefore debatable.

The optimistic first Five Year Plan proved to be a wise decision even if at first it has been privately considered as a wild flight of the imagination. The unrealistic targets galvanised people into action, more than orthodox targets would have done. Workers were also motivated through wage differentials reflecting skill, dedication and responsibility. Stalin maintained that targets had to be met at any cost. 'Shock workers' and 'shock brigades' showed the workers the way. Success was met with little congratulation, but failure could mean facing a penalty of disgrace, demotion and fines, or even arrest on the charge of sabotage. Stalin encouraged competition, and rival industrial groups fought each other ruthlessly for success. Workers worked to the bone with very little in return. Living standards in the cities were extremely low. Peasants flocked to the cities with working class numbers doubling during the first five year plan. Unemployment disappeared in the cities, and industry took on more workers than planned.

This is rather a vague paragraph. Ayesha should signal that she is now turning from the topic of agriculture to that of industry. She should mention that the first five year plan in industry focused on the heavy industries, coal, iron and steel, where the target was to double output, a target which was in fact met in four years, or so Stalin claimed. New factories, dams, power plants and new industrial towns were built, often by prisoners in labour camps. Ayesha should be more specific, and mention some of these developments by name, for instance the new industrial town of Manitogorsk in the Urals, and the Dnieper dam which created hydro-electric power to develop the older industrial centre of the Donetz basin.

Further comment is needed too to tie all this up to the question, so that Ayesha can make it clear that she still has its key words 'method' and 'extent' in mind. She might comment more specifically on the ruthlessness of Stalin's methods; his absolute control over the lives of the workers and total lack of concern for either their welfare or their rights. She might point out how far from the ideals of socialism these methods were, a point which could be made too about the competition and rivalry which she tells us Stalin fostered in his workers. Socialism is about co-operation; Stalin's methods set workers against each other. It is this kind of comment which lifts a satisfactory answer into a good one. What you need to do is stand back for a moment from the narrative of what happened, and make a comment which linkes up what you have been saying to the terms of the question. By what methods did Stalin effect economic and social change? A satisfactory answer like Ayesha's demonstrates that they were ruthless methods, which do not square with common humanity. A good answer will go deeper and say also that they were methods which do not square with his professed socialism either.

The second Five Year Plan did not set such demanding and unrealistic targets. Accordingly it was over-fulfilled in general by three per cent. Stalin recognised the need for great social change in the Soviet Union. Forging peasants into industrial workers proved to be a painful process. Although full employment was achieved, peasants tended to move from job to job. So in 1931 Stalin imposed the first of his draconian employment laws. Prison sentences were imposed on anyone who violated labour discipline. In August 1932 the theft of state or collective farm property became a capital offence. In November 1932, absenteeism, if only for a day, led to instant dismissal, and the internal passport was introduced in December 1932 to restrict movement.

Stalin and his planners were disappointed with the slow rise in labour productivity, the miserable housing conditions, and the shortages of food. Stalin was forced to ration bread, and by 1940, forty million people relied on bread rationing from 'centralised sources', and a further ten million from local sources. Many could not obtain ration cards and the black market flourished. Prices soared.

Stalin put a great emphasis on training which led to the technical revolution of the 1930s. Science and technology acquired a dominant position. Students were educated to instruct the generally technically backward workforce. Education became one of the largest growth industries in the Soviet Union.

Ayesha only touches on the huge increase in education, with a drive to build more schools, universities and technical institutes, which took place in the 1930s. Illiteracy, which had been widespread particularly amongst the peasantry, was decreased dramatically. The other side of the education coin was the indoctrination through which people were persuaded that Stalin was concerned, benign, and above all, right. The existence of Stalin's vast propaganda machine, which included censorship of the press as well as prescribed topics for education, was certainly an agent of social change. Free health care (Stalin needed a fit work force) was also introduced. You could also suggest that a new class of party bureaucrats was created, many of them, as Ayesha suggested in her introduction, like Stalin, corrupt and ruthless.

There can be no question of the scale of Stalin's achievement in completely transforming one of the largest nations of the world within such a short timespan. He saw the potential of a backward nation, and ruthlessly transformed it into a world super power. The price paid for such an achievement was, however, enormous. Stalin's lack of compassion for the welfare and livelihood of millions of people is the mark of a brutal and sadistic man. A vast number of Kulaks and their families, no less than five million people, mysteriously disappeared, either dying of starvation or malnutrition or forced to spend the rest of their lives in misery imprisoned in forced labour camps. The Russian people despite working their fingers to the bone were forced to live in squalid overcrowded industrial slums wondering where their next meal would come from. At the end of the 1930s Stalin addressed the Soviet people, 'Life has become better comrades. Life has become more joyous.'

In her conclusion Ayesha quite rightly focuses on the keyword 'extent'. She concludes that economic and social change in the 1930s had been immense, but that the methods of achieving it involved an unacceptable level of suffering in the Soviet population. Once again she misses the opportunity to suggest that Stalin's methods ran counter to the ideals of the Bolshevik revolution, which might lead on to a very brief discussion of whether ends can ever justify means. Does the fact that the USSR did become a powerful economic nation, and that standards of living did eventually rise, justify the human cost involved? This is not an easy question to answer, and is a moral one rather than a historical one, but it never hurts to demonstrate that you are aware that such questions can be posed, even if you don't feel able to offer an answer.

Having spent a comparatively long time on the first Five Year Plan, Ayesha then rushes through the second, realising, perhaps, that though she has dealt with economic change, she has yet to say much about social change. Consequently she says less about the second half of the decade than about the first, which results in unbalanced coverage. Even when she appears to decide to address the issue of social change, she still concentrates too much on economic change. Perhaps she needs to define to herself what social change really means. I would suggest that social change involves fairly large scale changes in people's class, lifestyle, standards of living, education and aspirations. Ayesha clearly has some of this in mind, but she approaches the issue of social change rather obliquely. It is easy to do this unconsciously, if you have a fear at the back of your mind that if you are too specific about something you might reveal that your idea of it is wrong! Consequently Ayesha slides around social change, without ever coming right out and saying where she thinks social change took place. Certainly it happened in the channelling of peasants into the towns to become industrial workers, which affected their whole lifestyle and class consciousness. Life as a factory worker rather than a peasant would have involved considerably more regimentation under Stalin's employment laws than life on the land, and little more independence. On the other hand there may have been more sense of solidarity with the large number of other industrial workers, and more opportunity for advancement and education.

It is a shame that instead of seeing these deeper implications, Ayesha has fallen back on cliche again ('working their fingers to the bone', 'wondering where their next meal was coming from'). Nor does she comment on the bitter irony of the words she quotes from Stalin at the end of her essay, which history has rendered more revealing of the extent of Stalin's inhuman manipulation of the Soviet people than of the truth.

In general, I feel that this was a sound essay. It could have been structured better so as to achieve more balance. Ayesha might, for instance, instead of approaching the 1930s chronologically, and then finding herself spending too long on the first Five Year Plan at the expense of the second and the third (which began in 1938), have chosen to take the period as a whole, dealing first with agriculture and then with industry.

There was a problem of selection in this essay. If you included all the material at your disposal you could probably write an essay more than twice as long as Ayesha's. Ayesha might have mentioned, for example, the incentives introduced in the second Five Year Plan, and the mining hero Stakhanov, who was supposed to have cut 102 tons of coal in a single shift (a figure since discredited). She might have said more about consumer goods, which always came second to heavy industry, leaving a legacy of consumer shortages which we still hear about today. She might have mentioned the need in the second half of the decade to spend more on defence in the face of the threat of German re-armament. But Ayesha's selection of material does show an appreciation of what is important for this question, and an understanding of Stalin's Russia, both of which will carry her a long way.

Jessica Saraga has wide experience as a sixth-form teacher and examiner.

Index